W9-BVQ-311

Math Is Language Too

NCTE Editorial Board: Jacqueline Bryant, Kermit Campbell, Gail Wood, Xin Liu Gale, Sarah Hudelson, Jackie Swensson, Gerald R. Oglan, Helen Poole, Karen Smith, Chair, ex officio, Zarina M. Hock, ex officio

Math Is Language Too

Talking and Writing in the Mathematics Classroom

Phyllis Whitin
Queens College, CUNY

David J. Whitin
Queens College, CUNY

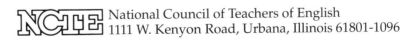

National Council of Teachers of English
1111 W. Kenyon Road, Urbana, Illinois 61801-1096

National Council of Teachers of Mathematics
1906 Association Drive, Reston, Virginia 20191-9988

Figure 1-2 and parts of Chapter 3 appeared previously. Reprinted with permission from *The Teaching and Learning of Algorithms in School Mathematics,* copyright 1998 by the National Council of Teachers of Mathematics.

Prepress Services: Electronic Imaging

Manuscript Editor: Jessica Creed

Production Editor: Rita D. Disroe

Interior Design: Doug Burnett

Cover Design: Pat Mayer

Left cover photograph courtesy of the authors.

Right cover photograph © Joel Brown. Used by permission.

NCTE Stock Number: 21349-3050

© 2000 by the National Council of Teachers of English. All rights reserved. Printed in the United States of America.

It is the policy of NCTE in its journals and other publications to provide a forum for the open discussion of ideas concerning the content and the teaching of English and the language arts. Publicity accorded to any particular point of view does not imply endorsement by the Executive Committee, the Board of Directors, or the membership at large, except in announcements of policy, where such endorsement is clearly specified.

Library of Congress Cataloging-in-Publication Data

Whitin, Phyllis.
    Math is language too: talking and writing in the mathematics classroom/Phyllis Whitin, David J. Whitin.
        p. cm.
    Includes bibliographical references.
    ISBN 0-8141-2134-9 (pbk.)
    1. Mathematics—Study and teaching. I. Whitin, David Jackman, 1947– II. Title.

QA8.7.W48 2000
510'.71—dc21

99-087801

Table of Contents

Authors' Note

One reason we wrote this book is to demonstrate the common beliefs about learning that cut across the fields of mathematics and language. Historically, members of national organizations have had little communication with each other. Each traditionally has held its own conferences and published its own research. However, it has become apparent that they are all united by a growing body of research. Some of the core beliefs of this research include valuing learners as constructors of their own knowledge; recognizing the social nature of how learners construct that knowledge; and encouraging the use of multiple avenues (writing, talking, drawing, building models) for expressing understandings. These common beliefs unite us as educators and push us to do more collaborative work.

This collaboration has already started. These national organizations have begun to hold joint conferences. They are also continuing to publish more books together. This book is unique because it is the first joint publication by National Council of Teachers of Mathematics and National Council of Teachers of English. We are honored to be a part of this growing collaborative movement.

Introduction

Setting and Class Composition

The stories in this book describe events that took place over a period of four years in a fourth-grade classroom. Each class was heterogeneously grouped and self-contained. The population of the school reflected a middle class and professional community. Some children were remedial readers, and others were identified as learning-disabled or gifted learners. Despite differences in ability, even in small groups, the children worked together, thus confirming the value of diverse grouping, which is one of the underlying principles of this book. We believe that each individual learner has something to offer a group. Some children have a sophisticated number sense; others have an aptitude for spatial relations. Still other children show a talent for expressing ideas through drawings, making personal connections, inventing ways to describe ideas, or linking mathematical ideas to stories or scientific investigations. We have witnessed again and again the insights that children of varying academic abilities have given each other. Many of the children whose stories we tell in this book would not be recognized for their mathematical aptitude in the traditional sense, yet each has contributed to the growth of our mathematical communities.

The Logistics of Classroom Organization

Readers will note references to Phyllis and David throughout this book. Phyllis Whitin taught fourth-grade at Dutch Forth Elementary School, in Irmo, South Carolina. David Whitin taught elementary education at the University of South Carolina and spent several hours each week in Phyllis's classroom. He was present for most of the experiences described in this book.

All students participated in each of the experiences described in the following chapters. Usually, we teachers would introduce an investigation to the whole group. Next, the children would explore the materials or the problem that was posed. The children's desks were grouped in clusters of four or six in order to facilitate informal talk during this work time. Typically, we teachers circulated around the room, taking notes about the children's discoveries and difficulties, as well as talking with individual children about their thinking. It was often during these conversations that we found misunderstandings that needed to be addressed with the whole group, or helpful strategies to bring to the class's attention. We also used these conversations to give children individual attention and encouragement, and to invite more shy class members to share their ideas with their peers.

Having time for small-group sharing gave everyone a greater chance to voice an opinion. However, we believe that gathering the group together for a whole-class discussion is equally important. Building a mathematical community is dependent upon the belief that all members of the group have important ideas to offer. Sometimes we would stop an investigation midway and review the discoveries that had been made so far. We often listed key observations on the board. Then, when children returned to their individual and group work, they could draw upon these ideas. This strategy helped support the more reluctant writers, but it often led the more capable students to connect ideas as well. We found that shuttling back and forth between small- and large-group discussions kept the momentum of an exploration going.

Most children were attentive during whole class discussions. Although there were times when individual students "tuned out," we were able to address this reality of classroom life in different ways. On rare occasions, we separated a disruptive child from the group. Usually, however, we had "intermissions" during a discussion in which all children wrote about their current thinking in their journals. In this way we placed the responsibility for learning on all the children, making them more able to participate in class discussion. Often we listed children's ideas on the board during a discussion. One of the acceptable journal entries included copying someone's insight from the board and giving a personal reaction, i.e., "I like Megan's idea because she shows why you need to regroup the tens."

We did not require this writing simply to keep students busy. Experts in the field of writing have long recognized that the act of writing itself is generative. Often while writing one comment, the children would develop a new idea. Additionally, the children were aware that their journal entries contributed to their mathematics grade. We felt that if talking and writing were important enough for us to spend large portions of time on them, then we should include them as part of the evaluative measures. Phyllis evaluated each entry holistically. She gave a *plus* for an entry that extended or explained an idea with clear details, a *check* for a simple but adequate comment, and a *minus* for a minimal comment. At the end of each grading period, she counted the proportion of pluses, checks, and minuses to arrive at a traditional letter journal grade. Quizzes also included writing, even for computation examples. Children could only earn a grade of *A* if they solved problems accurately and explained them clearly in writing.

During some conversations there were children who clearly had difficulty understanding a strategy or a concept. Sometimes we worked with these children individually, at other times we paired children to work together or addressed a common misconception as a whole class. What we chose to do often depended on the extent of the confusion and the nature of the misunderstanding. In a similar way, we worked individually with children who had the interest and capability to go beyond the given problem to pursue further relationships in more detail.

Mathematics and the Context of the Rest of the Day

The writing and talking described in this book reflect the belief that each person is a worthy member of the classroom community. This belief lays the foundation for all the experiences we plan for the children. The chief rule of the classroom is "No put downs." We cannot develop an environment that freely allows risk-taking if children are afraid of being criticized. From the very first day of class, we make it clear that even teasing, which some children might consider playful in other contexts, is not acceptable. We read aloud *Crow Boy* (Yashima, 1955, 1976), a story about a child who is ridiculed until he has the opportunity to reveal his unique talents. As a class we discuss the detrimental effects of teasing and suggest ways to search out and appreciate the gifts of each person. The class then looks for ways to collaborate in supportive ways throughout the day. In writing class, the children rehearse positive ways to suggest revisions for each other's stories. Children often read with partners or in groups, and they share their unique interpretations of literature and strategies for reading. In science, the children are encouraged to solve and extend problems by entertaining each group member's ideas and then testing them out. In all these areas we teachers emphasize how children can positively interact with each other and learn from each other's special talents.

We also strive to develop a spirit of inquiry across all subjects. After children read a story, they often analyze an author's style and look for similar themes across stories. In social studies we ask the children to be "social studies detectives" by figuring out why people settled in certain geographical locations. In science the children spend time developing their own questions to pursue, or discussing the *why* behind scientific relationships. This common emphasis on inquiry supports children to use ideas from one subject area to explain their work in another. For example, children used the concept of population density to describe the large number of factors in a composite number; another child compared a pattern in geometry to the layering of sedimentary rock.

Constraints of Time and District Mandates

One of the tensions that we as teachers face is how to use our instructional time. Talking and writing take time, and we can't talk and write about everything. Sometimes children write about how they solved only a few problems, but at other times they solve a larger set of computational problems with no writing at all. At a certain point we feel that the children simply need more time to practice basic computational skills. On some occasions we extend the time for discussion because the children raise important ideas that we teachers had not originally considered. At other times we curtail the conversation because we feel that the major ideas have been covered, and no new strategies are being offered. We are the first to admit that we are not perfect in the way we manage our time. It is usually in hindsight that we realize some missed opportunities. Nevertheless, by reflecting upon these teaching decisions, we become more attuned to the cues of children and more conscious of our role to better capitalize upon the benefits of talking and writing.

Many teachers today feel frustrated by tight mandates dictated by their school or their district. There were times when we, too, felt those pressures. However, despite the existence of a list of required topics or textbook, there is always the freedom for a teacher to ask questions that allow children to express their thinking. Even a computational answer can be followed with, "Why does that make sense to you?" or "Who has another way to solve the same problem?" as well as, "Who can tell Jenny what they appreciate about her explanation?" These are the steps that help to build a mathematical community.

Our Intentions for Using This Book

Although this book offers numerous activities to use with children, it is not meant to be a prescriptive activity book. Instead, it is a book about how to build a mathematical community where all voices are honored. It is a book about how writing and talking can be used to uplift these individual voices, and to enrich the collective pool of mathematical ideas. The activities that we plan for children may change, but the principles of learning do not. This book, then, is an invitation to you, as readers, to act upon these principles in ways that seem appropriate for your students and your own classroom community. Your stories will be different, but it is this diversity that benefits us all.

Talking, Writing, and Mathematical Thinking

Figure 1-1

When second-grade teacher Nancy Kerr asked her students at the beginning of the year to write about what mathematics was, Justin wrote and drew Figure 1-1.

Justin's brief commentary captures many of the dysfunctional beliefs that children come to associate with mathematics: only right answers count; teachers tell you how to get those right answers; working alone is the best way to improve one's competence.

This book focuses on ways to empower learners to think for themselves. It is a book about respecting children as sense-makers. We feel that there is no belief that can more radically change the teaching and learning of mathematics than this one. For if we view children as sense-makers, then we must also see them as story

Figure 1-1 originally appeared in "Ice Numbers and Beyond: Language Lessons for the Mathematics Classroom." *Language Arts* 74, no. 2 (February 1997): 108–15.

tellers, language creators, and problem-posers; we must value their background experiences and interests because we know these are important lenses for viewing their meaning-making efforts; we must value their stories because we know that stories are the way they frame their understanding of the world; we must value the many ways that they solve and pose problems because we see these as reflections of children's personal ways of thinking. In short, we must value their language, questions, descriptions, observations, and stories because these are windows into the process of how our students construct meaning. If we really view children as sense-makers, then we are required to step inside their shoes and view the world as they see it—through children's eyes.

As professional educators, we know that good teaching does not just happen through children's eyes alone. We must also take what we know about successful teaching and learning and use this knowledge to capitalize and extend children's current understand-ings of their world. As teachers of children, we must be close observ-ers, keen listeners, and skillful questioners. However, we must also be reflective learners ourselves; we know that our own observations of children reflect our own beliefs about good learning. In this book we recognize sense making as the cornerstone of this belief system. We see mathematics and language as ways for learners to make sense of their world. Sense making in mathematics involves the strategic use of concepts, strategies, and skills. Concepts are the bedrock of mathematical thinking; they enable learners to view the world in a mathematical way (Steen, 1990; Paulos, 1988; Mills, O'Keefe, & Whitin, 1996): How long will it take me to complete this task (time)? What is the likelihood that I can get tickets for the concert (probability)? What is the cost of carpeting this room (area, money)? Strategies are "planful" ways to carry out the given task, such as estimating the cost of groceries in the basket; matching socks when doing the laundry; or counting the votes in a class election. Skills enable learners to obtain more specific answers, such as calcu-lating the exact cost of those groceries or those square yards of carpet.

Writing and talking are ways that learners can make their mathematical thinking visible. Both writing and talking are tools for collaboration, discovery, and reflection. For instance, talking is fluid; it allows for a quick interchange of ideas; learners can modify, elaborate and generate ideas in a free-wheeling manner. Talking also allows for the quick brainstorming of many possible ideas, thereby giving the group many directions to consider. It is this "rough-draft" talk that allows peers and teachers a window into each other's thinking. As we talk with freshly fashioned ideas in our minds, we all witness the birth of still further ideas. Sharing partially formed ideas builds a willingness to live with the tentative and the provisional, an important dimension of a risk-taking stance (Lampert, 1990).

Writing shares many of the qualities of talking, but it has some unique characteristics of its own, such as creating a record of our thinking that we can analyze and reflect upon. Talking and writing enable learners to develop a personal voice. For example, after spending most of his fourth-grade year writing and talking about mathematical ideas, Jonathan sketched his interpretation of their benefits (Figure 1-2).

Jonathan showed that writing and talking are generative when he wrote, "You get more ideas." His repeated statement, "People get to know you," demonstrates his understanding that writing and talking are ways that learners can stamp their personal signatures on their mathematical thinking. Writing and talking are usually done with others in mind; children need the opportunity to share mathematical ideas in these ways so they can express what they know with a real audience.

When children have regular invitations to write and talk about mathematics in open-ended ways, they soon recognize they can discover new ideas in the process. The following fourth-grade students wrote about this potential. Danielle wrote: [Conversations] helped me develop more ideas, and the more ideas, the more interested I got." Conversations with others draws learners deeper into an issue or problem. Lauren emphasized the same point when she wrote: "My picture shows that when one person raises their hand to say something everyone in the class raises their hand with a new idea" (Figure 1-3).

Meredith wrote: "Our ideas give others bigger ideas." Stephanie sketched the power of collaboration and discovery: "This sketch shows how when no one raises their hand everybody's brain light is off. This sketch shows how when someone raises their hand everyone's brain light is on" (Figure 1-4).

All of these children highlight one of Vygotsky's (1978) main ideas: talking does not merely reflect thought but it generates new thoughts and new ways to think. As members of a collaborative learning community the children are learning that together they can go further than any of them could go alone.

Writing is also a tool for discovery in mathematics. Lily wrote: "It (writing in mathematics) teaches me how to learn. When I write I get lots of ideas of what else I want to say." William reiterated this same idea: "You get more ideas. You get your imagination going." Jenny also reflected about the magic of discovering in writing: "When I write I get more ideas. See, I know what I'm going to write, but by the time I get to a part, I get a new idea." This potential of

Figure 1-2

writing and talking to discover new thoughts and ideas is one of the most important benefits for the teaching and learning of mathematics.

Sharing mathematical ideas through writing and talking builds a strong community of learners. Tiffany wrote of this mutual

Figure 1-3

Figure 1-4

Figure 1-5

support by comparing it to the caring of a family: "They share ideas and get along. Have good long conversations with each other and good ideas. We are like a family because we help each other. . . . And that is the way that this class works, and we are proud of it" (Figure 1-5).

The risks that learners are willing to venture in mathematics are a reflection of the kind of community in which they live. Creating a community that supports the expression of mathematical ideas in many different forms is an important dimension of this risk-taking stance. In summary, writing and talking help to build a collaborative community that enables children to generate ideas, develop a personal voice, and reflect upon their current understandings.

The Teacher's Role in Building a Mathematical Community

National organizations in the field of language and mathematics have recognized the value of writing and talking as tools for understanding. The National Council of Teachers of Mathematics Standards recognizes this important role of language when it lists "learning to communicate mathematically" as one of the primary goals for all students. It advocates the development of "problem situations in which students have the opportunity to read, write, and discuss ideas in which the use of the language of mathematics becomes natural. As students communicate their ideas, they learn to clarify, refine, and consolidate their thinking" (1989, p.6). It proposes that children have numerous opportunities to "realize that representing, discussing, reading, writing, and listening to mathematics are a vital part of learning and using mathematics" (1989, p. 26). Likewise, the National Council of Teachers of English has been advocating the importance of using reading, writing, and talking for real purposes. In fact, both organizations emphasize a common set of beliefs about what constitutes good learning (Mills, O'Keefe & Whitin, 1996): (1) Learners are active constructors of their own knowledge; they are meaning-makers who are always making sense of problem situations by connecting them to what they already know; (2) Learners can represent their ideas through many forms of expression. Oral language, written language, mathematics, as well as drama, art, and music, are important channels for learners to express what they know about the world. (3) Learners construct knowledge in a social context. The way that learners construct what they know is influenced by the social situation in which they find themselves.

As natural as this potential is, it is not realized without the conscious decision-making of the teacher. How then do teachers build a community of mathematical thinkers who have opportunities to construct knowledge, express ideas, and share personal interpretations? The following list offers some strategies that we have developed for putting these beliefs into action:

1. *Highlight the process.* Children need to see that mathematics is more than a series of right-or-wrong answers. In order for them to value the process of mathematical thinking we have posed questions such as these:

"How did you solve that problem?"

"Did anyone solve it another way?"

"Tell us about what was going through your mind when you were working on this problem."

When we first invite children to explain their thinking at the beginning of the year, they sometimes look a bit hesitant, fearful that their answers are wrong. Many children have been conditioned by past classroom experiences to describe their thinking only when their answers were incorrect. By encouraging children to express their thinking in all circumstances, even when their answers might be the predicted response, we find that children have much to show us about their sense-making efforts.

We have also encouraged children to answer their own questions. Instead of all questions being directed to and answered by the teacher, we turn the questions back to the children: "Who can answer Deidre's question about this pattern?" In this way the conversation does not become a paired interchange between individual children and the teacher (Wood, 1998; Schwartz, 1996). It also demonstrates that individual questions are owned by the group and that everyone has a responsibility for each other's thinking and understanding.

2. *Recognize the thinking of others.* To build a community of learners who are willing to share their strategies and ideas with others, we must provide opportunities for people to recognize the thinking of others in many different ways. At the beginning of the year we teachers set the example by saying such things as "I appreciate the way Sara used a drawing to show how she traded ten units for one ten because it helped to show her thinking in another way," or "I appreciate how Jon used the metaphor of an overflowing cup to describe an improper fraction (5/3) because it gave me a picture in my mind of what happens when there is a quantity greater than one whole." It is important to accompany the appreciation with a reason so that learners know specifically the thinking behind the recognition. After we publicly express our appreciation we invite the children to do the same: "Who else would like to share an appreciation with Sara?" or "What else do people appreciate about the way Jon described his answer?" If the children have nothing else to contribute we usually add another appreciation ourselves before we ask other children to share.

We share other kinds of appreciations as well and invite the children to do likewise:

"Who would like to share an appreciation to someone who helped them during our work time today?"

"Who would like to share an appreciation to someone for asking a question that helped you grow as a learner?"

"Who would like to share an appreciation to someone who shared a comment, idea or suggestion that helped you understand some of this math in a new way?"

The focus of these appreciations is how others have helped us *grow*, not merely on what we liked in some general way. For instance, when Jonathan shared that his strategy for solving $10 - 7 = ?$ was to think of it as $7 + ? = 10$ we asked for specific appreciations. A response such as, "I liked how Jonathan solved it in a new way" is not specific enough. Our reply is, "What made it a new way for you?" A child then elaborates, "Well, he made the subtracting problem into an adding problem and that was easier for me to think about." Not only does this specificity help Jonathan know what part of his thinking was appreciated, but it also contributes to the class's understanding of the relationship between addition and subtraction.

As teachers we do not want to hide our intentions from children. We want children to recognize the potential of how a collaborative community nurtures individual growth (Borasi, et al., 1998). We believe that when learners share their thinking with the group we all benefit from hearing different explanations, viewing different modes of expression, and reconsidering alternative ways to interpret a problem. If we really believe in these benefits of collaborative learning, then we must invite appreciations that highlight this potential.

In addition to inviting public appreciations there are two other strategies we have used to recognize the thinking of others: (1) the traveling overhead transparency; and (2) the naming of strategies. We invite a child to take an overhead transparency home one night and record (with written narrative and pictures) how he or she solved one of the homework problems. The next day that child explains his or her thinking with the class. Knowing that they are going to share their thinking the following day makes children even more reflective about their problem-solving efforts. Sharing their work on an overhead lends an aura of importance to the event as well. The child in charge is also responsible for answering questions from anyone who had difficulty with the problem. When children finish their sharing we invite a few of them to offer appreciations as a way to conclude the session. The children enjoy the deserved recognition and see again the value we place in understanding each other's thinking.

The second way that we value children's thinking is to name a mathematical strategy in honor of the child who invented it. For instance, when Laura Jane solved 9 + 7 she explained, "I took one from the 7 and added it to the 9 to make a ten, and then I added ten and six and got 16. It's easier when I make a ten." The children tested out the strategy on other facts for 9 (9 + 4, 9 + 5, 9 + 6 and so on) and found it to be useful in all these cases as well. To honor her thinking we asked Laura Jane what she wanted to call this strategy and she said "the nines strategy." From that day forward we referred to that strategy as "Laura Jane's nines strategy" and added it to a master list of strategies that we had posted in the room. Throughout the year the children would use Laura Jane's name when referring to this strategy; this ritual of naming not only honored the individual child but emphasized the social origins of the class's mathematical ideas.

3. *Honor surprise.* It is important to cultivate a classroom atmosphere in which surprise is acknowledged and valued. At the beginning of the year some children seem reluctant to share surprising observations with the class. (Our hunch is that their past instructional history has taught them that if they are surprised then they were

either not listening carefully to the teacher or they did not understand the teacher's directions.) However, if we view learners as respected sense-makers and meaning-makers, then surprise is a very healthy sign; it means that children are trying to make sense of a given situation and explain certain unexpected results. For instance, Danny used some blocks to show that 7 was an odd number because he could not build two towers of equal height. He later proved that 17 was also odd and predicted that 27, 37, 47, and so on, would also be odd. When his teacher (David) asked him about 70 he predicted it also would be odd because it had a 7. However, when other classmates showed that they could divide 70 into two equal parts, Danny had to admit that 70 was indeed even—and he was surprised! He was puzzled that some numbers had 7s and were odd and yet other numbers (like 70) were even. This surprise led him to examine the numbers more closely and with help from his classmates he saw that the critical difference lay in the one's place. As teachers we can honor surprise by asking children regularly, "Did anything surprise you today as you worked?" We can then capitalize on the potential of surprise by asking further, "*Why* was that surprising to you?" and "How can we explain what happened?" Since surprise is the catalyst that causes learners to revise their current theories and explain the results in a new way, it is important for teachers to encourage children to make public their surprises. If learners expect surprise they'll find it. If they don't, they won't. When children are valued as respected detectives, they will view surprise as part of their daily work.

Teachers are contributing members of the learning community and they, too, must share their surprises with the class. Sometimes the strategies that children share are surprising to the teacher. When a student shared that her strategy for figuring out $12 - 5$ was to add the 5 and the 2 (from the 12) to get 7, the teacher (David) and the class were all quite amazed. She explained that the strategy worked for other combinations as well: $13 - 5 = 5 + 3 = 8$, and $14 - 5 = 4 + 5 = 9$. David and the children quickly tested out this strategy on other problems and found that it only worked when subtracting 5 in the subtrahend. However, the surprise led us all to wonder: why does this strategy work? David needed unifix cubes to act out the problem for himself, and only then could he understand why the strategy worked: by renaming the 12 as $5 + 5 + 2$ he could then subtract either one of the 5s and still have the other 5 left over, which he then could add to the 2 to make 7. It was because the 10 was composed of two 5s that the strategy worked. Here again surprise led us all down the road of unexpected, yet rewarding, mathematical understanding.
4. *Invite reflection.* We have had children keep math journals and

asked them to record their reflections about most investigations in this journal. We tape a set of questions on the inside front cover of each journal as suggestions for writing:

1) What do you notice?
2) What do you find interesting?
3) What patterns do you see?
4) What surprises you?
5) What do you predict? Why?
6) What do your findings make you wonder?
7) What does this remind you of?

The children are not required to respond to each question every day. In fact, some questions are sometimes more appropriate for one experience than another; mathematical experiences that are rich in patterns invite a lot of reflection on patterns and possible predictions about those patterns, while a series of child-generated story problems might invite more reflection on the intriguing nature of the problems themselves. However, having this wide range of questions available for each experience allows children the opportunity to respond in many different ways.

We teachers have intentionally posed open-ended questions so that children have the freedom to respond to any interesting feature of the problem. We did not want to narrow the range of responses but instead sought a list of questions that would make each journal unique and different. Past experiences showed that even the question, "What did you learn today?" was not an effective one for eliciting a diversity of responses. Children tended to write about what they did rather than reflect on the nature of the learning that occurred. Responses such as, "We used the base ten blocks today and learned how to do some trading" did not make public the children's thinking. The question, "Do you have any questions?" was also not helpful because children were reluctant to admit questions, especially in the area of mathematics. The word *wonder* seemed to better capture this same spirit. *Wonder* seemed to be a less threatening word; the children had little previous school association with this word, which conjured up a non-judgemental invitation to extend the experience in new ways.

We included the last question, "What does this remind you of?" because we found that children naturally described observations in metaphorical terms. For instance, Danny was circling the multiples of four and eight on the hundred square chart. He noticed that each multiple of eight was always circled twice and reasoned that multiples of four have the multiples of eight inside them. He then shared a personal analogy: "Four is like eight's little sister; she follows him wherever he goes." Danny had a younger sister and probably drew upon some personal experiences to construct this wonderful connection. (Other examples of metaphors will be shared throughout the book to illustrate the potential this question has for inviting interesting mathematical insights.)

The list of questions also reflects the values and beliefs that we hold as teachers. We want to encourage children to look closely, find interesting things, detect patterns, predict outcomes, pursue surprises, and pose wonders. The questions we ask and the language we use define who we are as a classroom community (Lampert, 1990). We have come to realize the importance of the verbs that we use in our classroom community to convey the intentions of our mathematical decisions. Some of the verbs that we use most often with children include: *explore, investigate, invent, discover, revise,* and *pretend.* They can be found in the following challenges and questions:

> What did you find when you *explored* that pattern?
> What is another way we can *investigate* this problem?
> *Invent* a strategy to solve that problem.
> How did you go about *discovering* this relationship?
> How can you *revise* your theory to include this new information?
> *Pretend* that the problem is slightly different and see what happens.

The language that we use to describe our intentions sets the parameters for what is possible. As teachers, we have come to pay closer attention to our language because we know it sets the tone for our classroom climate.

We have described some of our basic beliefs about good mathematical learning and have outlined some initial strategies for supporting this belief system in the classroom. Now we turn to two classroom scenarios that show in more detail how these beliefs and strategies look in operation.

Who Owns the Questions? Who Owns the Solution?

An unexpected classroom event one September provided us with an opportunity to look closely at how we respond to children's questions. We had spent several days solving subtraction problems with base ten blocks. (As will be discussed in depth in Chapter 3, the children used the terminology of *unit* for the ones, *longs* for tens, and *flats* for 100 - square centimeter pieces.) On this day Phyllis asked the children to build the number 350 with blocks on their desks. She then asked them to remove (or subtract) 145 from this collection and describe their thinking process in their journals. After a few minutes, Phyllis asked the students to share the strategies that they used to arrive at their answers. Megan raised her hand, a worried look clouding her face. Glancing around her table, she admitted, "I got 105, but everyone around me got 205."

"Tell us what you did to get 105," Phyllis suggested.

Megan answered, "I crossed everything out on the top number."

$$
\begin{array}{cc}
\overset{2\ 4\ 10}{\cancel{350}} & \overset{4\ 10}{3\cancel{50}} \\
-\ 145 & -145 \\
\hline
105 & 205 \\
\end{array}
$$

(Megan's Solution)   (Other Children's Solutions)

Phyllis was pleased that Megan had taken the risk to share her different answer with the class but she did not want Megan to focus solely on the solution to this one problem. Rather she wanted her to look more generally at the reasons for regrouping. Phyllis thought that having several other children discuss their reasoning might help Megan understand the process in a more general way. Yet, already several children looked uninterested. She doubted that the majority of the class would invest energy into trying to understand Megan's thinking, suspecting that these children considered Megan's problem to be a solitary one, and that they were neither part of the problem nor part of the solution. On the spur of the moment, Phyllis decided to involve everyone simultaneously in Megan's present dilemma. She asked Megan's permission to have everyone consider this issue further, and then turned to the class to continue the conversation.

"That's a confusing problem," Phyllis began. "In this class people have lots of different ways to solve problems. I want all of you to think hard about Megan's problem, and to write Megan a response in your journals. In your own way explain to Megan why you don't have to trade flats, or cross out the hundreds place, in this problem. Then Megan will call on several of the *teachers* in this room to hear their explanations." She copied Megan's written problem on the board (see Figure 1-6), and then asked the children to write Megan a response.

As it turned out, there were several children who had difficulty explaining the regrouping process to Megan. (Even having the right answer does not ensure understanding.) When it came time for Megan to call on some classmates, those who had had trouble writing a response listened for their own sake, as well as Megan's. Other children explained very clearly to Megan the difference between needing to regroup and not needing to regroup. These children learned from the experience, too, by mentally searching for a way to express their understanding. They were proud of their explanations and were eager to share with the group. By turning the problem back to the entire class, all the students had the opportunity to benefit from Megan's question. Involving everyone carried an implied message that all members of the class were committed to help each other. Having children assume this responsibility minimized the chances that children would criticize Megan for an inaccurate answer. Instead, the class shared a common goal of making sense of a confusing problem. Meanwhile, Megan's role had changed from being the person who made a mistake to being the leader of a discussion.

Sharing Understandings with a Classmate

These are some of the written responses that the children shared with Megan:

Megan, you do not have to take away a flat because you have enough longs left to take away the four from the other four. (Stephanie)

You do not have to take a flat because the longs do not need help! Sometimes you do, and sometimes you do not. (Jamie)

Megan, you don't have to take away a flat because then it wouldn't be in the hundreds and the answer would be 11 and it wouldn't make sense. (Tony)

[Tony's '11' refers to the tens place, which would be the difference of fifteen tens minus four tens. His response shows what would happen to the tens place if a hundred were broken down into tens and moved to the tens place.]

Megan, you don't have to take away an extra flat because you borrowed a long, so you can get units. If it was a 150 to 345 you would have to take the first one away! (Jessica)

The children's explanations highlighted some interesting points for Megan to consider. Stephanie emphasized the importance of only trading when it was necessary to do so; Tony reasoned that trading a one hundred for ten tens would result in too many tens in that column; Jamie and Jessica explained that trading is contextual, and that a problem like 345 – 150 *would* require the exchanging of a 100 piece. As children offered their ideas, Megan listened closely. Part way through the discussion, she broke into a grin. She told her friends that she now understood the difference in problems that needed a great deal of regrouping and those that did not. It was helpful that she had heard so many interpretations of the problem. The conversation also benefited Phyllis in another way. The students' comments had served as a window for assessment. By reading the journals and listening to the children talk, we adults could assess each child's understanding and appreciate the personal strategies of each individual.

After the discussion, Tiff, who had also been confused initially, added a comment in her journal. Her complete entry read:

> Megan, you don't have to take away a flat because. I can't help you because I don't get it either. And so I can't answer you. I am really, really sorry. I wish I could. Well, now I can answer you because I listened to everybody. The longs do not need help because they have enough but if they don't have enough you need to trade a flat. Thank you for understanding.

Tiff clearly regretted that she could not explain the process to her classmate at first. Listening to the many explanations not only helped Tiff to understand the problem herself, but it gave her the opportunity to fulfill the responsibility that she felt for the welfare of others.

As teachers, we were also intrigued with Megan's willingness to share her anomaly with the class. We asked her privately about the entire experience the following day. Megan explained, "I had never seen a problem where you didn't cross out everything." (In drill and practice exercises, similar problems are usually grouped together for "mastery.") "When I first saw the problem, I said, 'Oh, this is easy.' But when I got 105 I looked around and other people got 205, and I was confused. I said to myself, 'What happened?'"

Phyllis remarked, "Sometimes people see that they don't have the same answer as others, but they keep it to themselves. Tell me about how you decided to ask." Megan replied, "In this class everyone is a teacher. If I asked a question, more people could help." This conversation with Megan helped us value her growth as a risk-taker who was more willing now to seek support from her peers. She also grew in confidence because she realized that voicing her problem helped her classmates.

In this story the children rallied to support Megan as she made sense of a confusing subtraction problem. However, as the next story will show, there is no guarantee in any classroom that children (or adults!) will refrain from criticizing others at all times. We could have assumed that once the children learned about respect and responsibility, they would consistently treat one another in those ways throughout the year (as they had treated Megan on that September day). However, both children and adults can forget this most important lesson about courtesy in the busy whirlwind of classroom life. Although we did talk about our community rules throughout the year, an incident the following January needed our special attention.

Sustaining a Respect for Sense Making

Over the course of the year, the children regularly created mathematical story problems. Phyllis would select ten to fifteen of these problems and duplicate them for homework practice. On this occasion, the students generated some division problems for homework. The next day the author of each problem called on another child to answer the problem and then explain how he or she solved it. Craig called on Gaye to solve his problem: "There were 184 stickers. Half the stickers have a bird on them. How many stickers have birds on them?" Gaye replied "142." Before Craig had a chance to ask Gaye how she obtained that answer, several children uttered a sarcastic "Huh?" Phyllis was upset by their tone and responded, "I didn't like those 'huh's.' That was an obvious put-down tone, and I don't tolerate put-downs in this classroom. The 'huh' sounded like, 'Boy, that's a stupid answer.' It sounded like, 'My answer is right, so I'm better.' I am angry about the 'huh.' Gaye's answer made sense to her, and we need to know what she was thinking so we can understand her answer."

Phyllis then asked Gaye to explain her reasoning. Gaye pointed to the numerals of 184 and said, "Half of four is two, and half of eight is four, and I just brought down the one." Phyllis realized the wonderful thinking that Gaye's strategy entailed; she had found half of 84 was 42 but did not know what to do with the remaining digit. Phyllis explained that the one represented "100" and asked Gaye what was half of 100. Gaye replied "50" and then together they added the 42 to the 50 and got the answer of 92. The children were quite impressed with this alternative way to solve the problem.

Reflecting upon the Climate of Our Classroom

Phyllis then asked the children to reflect upon what had just happened: "What did we learn from this experience?" They talked together about Gaye's feelings and about the benefits of appreciating each child's thinking. After reflecting more about the incident that evening, Phyllis decided to ask the children to write about the conversation in their journals. The children's comments show a sensitivity to the implications that this incident had for the classroom community. James wrote that the conversation was beneficial because, "Gaye might not have tried to help out with homework anymore." Joseph wrote, "We really didn't show friendship," and Stephanie showed a concern for the future: "If Gaye had another good idea she might be afraid that people would be rude about it like they were." Jessica captured the tone of the conversation in a direct way: "I don't think people should judge your answer before your thinking." Jamie wrote about the value of alternative strategies: "That conversation was important because we can get different ideas and strategies when someone has a different answer." Tiffany reiterated this same point: "It is very rude because they might have a good explanation that might help you with another problem."

Tiffany also was concerned about Gaye's feelings: "It would hurt her feelings and make her feel unimportant." Nick compared the exploratory nature of good conversations to the opportunity to investigate a new fort for the first time. He also concluded his piece by relating the class' discussions of civil rights to this present issue:

> If Gaye didn't share her thinking we might have not understood; we just like to know everything. It's like you are at a new fort; you don't know what's there, so what do you do? Explore, find trails, look around, find things. The main topic is to explore; that is the challenge, that is the adventure. You have to EXPLORE. You just have to find out what she is thinking. If she knows some kind of math problem, and we don't know [how she solved it], she [won't be able to] help us with her thinking. You can't judge the skin or the voice. The inside is important, and the brain, that is important.

This brief classroom scenario highlights some of the important dimensions of a classroom community that we have mentioned earlier: honor surprise, value children as sense-makers, encourage a variety of ways to solve problems, and develop a climate that respects all learners. Phyllis's response to Gaye, "Tell us how you solved this problem," valued her as a sense-maker. And indeed Gaye's strategy made good sense once she had the opportunity to explain it. Phyllis's supportive response also demonstrated to the children the importance of honoring surprise. As teachers we need to show how to respond to an unexpected answer. We need to be curious enough to say, "That's interesting, tell us some more," and not dismiss it as careless or nonsensical. We need to seek out surprise, examine it, and learn from it.

Conclusion

Writing and talking enable learners to make their mathematical thinking visible. It is through writing and talking that teachers obtain a window into their students' thinking. Both writing and talking are tools for discovery, enabling learners to make new connections as they engage in the process. The fluid nature of talk allows for the quick brainstorming of many ideas while the permanent quality of writing provides an important trail of our children's thinking.

Teachers play a key role in capitalizing on these benefits of writing and talking. Part of this role involves establishing norms of classroom life that recognize and appreciate the reasoning of others; highlight the process of mathematical thinking as children use concepts, strategies, and skills in strategic ways; honor surprise as a natural and legitimate part of the learning process; and invite reflection and self-evaluation as avenues for personal growth. In these next three chapters we will show in more detail the benefits of writing and talking about mathematical ideas and the key role that teachers play in nurturing this development.

2 Experiences with Children's Literature

In Chapter 1, we discuss how the classroom climate sets the tone for what is possible in a community of learners. In this chapter we ask, "What are some specific experiences that can foster this supportive community?" If we take to heart the conditions that are outlined in Chapter 1, such as valuing questions, honoring surprise, and inviting reflection, then we must ask ourselves what experiences can we plan for the classroom that will enable us to emphasize these important conditions. We have found that sharing a piece of literature is a particularly powerful way to involve children as sense-makers and problem-solvers (Whitin & Whitin, 1997, in press). This chapter describes three ways to capitalize upon children's literature: as a vehicle to explore mathematical patterns, to understand large numbers, and to appreciate the meaning of mathematical vocabulary. In the experiences we describe, we have implemented strategies that invite open-ended responses, promote the exchange of ideas in a collaborative community, and encourage risk taking. In this way, we as teachers play an active role in nurturing the kind of learning environment we want to establish in our classrooms.

Using Children's Literature to Inspire a Mathematical Investigation

Most children love to hear stories read aloud. We have found that sharing children's literature with a mathematical theme can set a non-threatening tone for mathematics classrooms (Whitin & Wilde, 1992, 1995). One August we decided to begin the school year with *Two Ways to Count to Ten* (Dee, 1988). In this Liberian folk tale, the leopard king challenges the other animals in the forest to a contest for the rights of his succession. The object of the contest is to throw his hunting spear high in the air and count to ten before it hits the ground. Animal after animal fails in the task until the antelope steps forward. Amidst the taunting of the others, the antelope tosses the spear, calling, "Two, four, six, eight, ten!" The king admits that he had not specified *how* to count, and he rewards the antelope with his daughter's hand in marriage and the rights to the kingdom.

Portions of this chapter originally appeared in "Ice Numbers and Beyond: Language Lessons for the Mathematics Classroom." *Language Arts* 74, no. 2 (February 1997): 108–15.

Oral Response to the Story

The fourth-graders' reaction to the story was similar to other children with whom we have shared this book. When we asked for reactions to the story, several children suggested that they could count to 10 even faster than the antelope. "Five, ten!" or even faster, "Ten!" We then reversed the problem, asking the children to find ways to count even more slowly to 10. They suggested counting down from a higher number (200, 199, 198, . . .), counting by fractions (1/2, 1, 1 1/2. . .), and starting with negative numbers (−5, −4, −3. . .).

We devoted time for oral sharing for several reasons. First, part of enjoying a story aloud is reacting to it together. We also wanted the children to experience a variety of responses to the numerical challenge of counting quickly or slowly. Together we were building a fund of ideas in a playful way that supported risk taking. We pointed out how one idea had led to another, such as counting down from 100, and counting down from an even higher number, thereby setting the foundation for collaboration in other experiences. We were beginning to demonstrate to the children that people's ideas have social origins, and building an idea from someone else's is not cheating. We wanted the children to realize that together we had more ideas than any of us (including adults) would have developed alone. Finally, by providing time for oral rehearsal, we were preparing our students for what they would later write in their journals.

In this conversation, we needed to be mindful of the ways the children responded to each other as well. When someone suggested trying to count by 2s starting with one, Kyle protested, "You can't do that!" Our reaction was, "Well, let's try. . . . what if we didn't begin with two? One, three, five, seven. . . . are we counting by 2s? What do others think? Does this way count?" Our response intended to encourage the spirit of flexibility that we think is a healthy part of problem-solving. It is interesting that later, when we were talking about counting to eleven, it was Kyle who suggested starting with one. The original discussion encouraged him to explore a non-traditional solution to the problem.

Written Response to the Story

After our discussion, we asked the children to write in their journals. For this first experience, we simply asked them to record ways to count to 10 slowly or quickly, and give a reason why there are more ways to count to 10 than there are to count to 11. The children could use any of the ideas offered during our discussion or develop new ideas on their own. Some children did invent new solutions. For example, Maggie took the fraction idea (counting by halves) and extended it to counting by fourths.

Most of the children answered the second question, "Why are there more ways to count to 10 than there are ways to count to 11?" with the theory that even numbers have more ways than odd. We asked this question for two reasons: (1) we wanted to establish the idea that mathematicians are detectives who want to find out the reasons behind the results; (2) we also wanted to lay the groundwork for further investigations the next day. Does it hold true that all even numbers have more ways than odd? Do some even numbers have more ways than others? Can odd numbers ever have more than two ways? If so, which ones, and why? (Children might use calculators to investigate the skip-counting patterns of different numbers). Thus, the question that we posed initially, "Why are there more ways to count to 10 than 11?" was an invitation for children to offer a hypothesis. It is this cycle of sharing observations, proposing theories, and ferreting out evidence that supports children to be mathematical inquirers. Learners go further, and they discover more, if they talk and write in a collaborative community.

Counting and Exploring with Other Numbers

The following day we expanded our investigation to find ways to count to other numbers. Together the class listed all the ways to count to 12 (by 1s, 2s, 3s, 4s, 6s, and 12). Most of the children were not surprised that there were six ways to count to twelve by equal intervals, since many of them had predicted that even numbers would have more ways than odd numbers. We also discussed some of their other observations about these six arrangements of counting on. Next, we asked the children to copy the ways from the board, think about our conversation, and write in their journals, responding to some of the questions listed in Chapter 1. They then could explore patterns for numbers larger than 12. We left the questions open-ended so that the children could respond in many ways; risk-taking and diversity of response were two of our goals. The following children's journals reflect this diversity.

Maggie experimented by changing some of the guidelines of this invitation. She decided to count not by equal intervals but by an alternating sequence of 2s and 3s. She wrote: "If you're trying to get to twelve you can try a pattern of 2, 3, 2, 3, 2. If you start with 2 and not 3 it will work." She used number sequences to prove her case. $3 + \underline{2} = 5$, $5 + \underline{3} = 8$, $8 + \underline{2} = 10$, $10 + \underline{3} = 13$ does not reach 12 but the following sequence does: $2 + \underline{3} = 5$, $5 + \underline{2} = 7$, $7 + \underline{3} = 10$, $10 + \underline{2} = 12$. Maggie had challenged herself to play with this counting strategy in a new way. Her investigation was especially intriguing for us as teachers and we wondered: What other ways can we count to 12 using an alternating sequence of numbers? What if we tried a sequence of three numbers? We have found that when mathematical explorations are kept open-ended, we as teachers are often challenged ourselves as well.

Selita investigated the principle of commutativity in a unique way. As she studied the lists of numbers in her journal, she noticed that there were twelve numbers when counting by 1s, six when counting by 2s, four when counting by 3s, three when counting by 4s, and so forth (Figure 2-1).

Figure 2-1

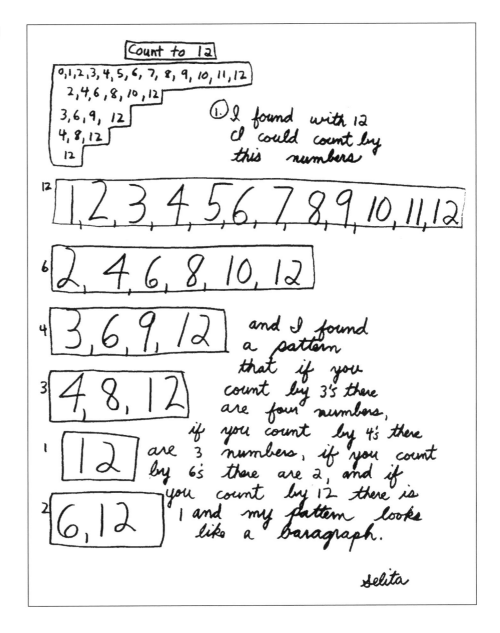

She wrote, "I found with twelve I could count by these numbers, and I found a pattern, that if you count by 3s there are four numbers, if you count by 4s there are three numbers, if you count by 6s there are two, and if you count by twelve there is one, and my pattern looks like a bar graph." Writing the sequences in horizontal bands helped to highlight the commutative relationship between these numbers.

Chelsea pursued the topic of odd and even numbers, but discovered a surprising new feature (Figure 2-2).

Figure 2-2

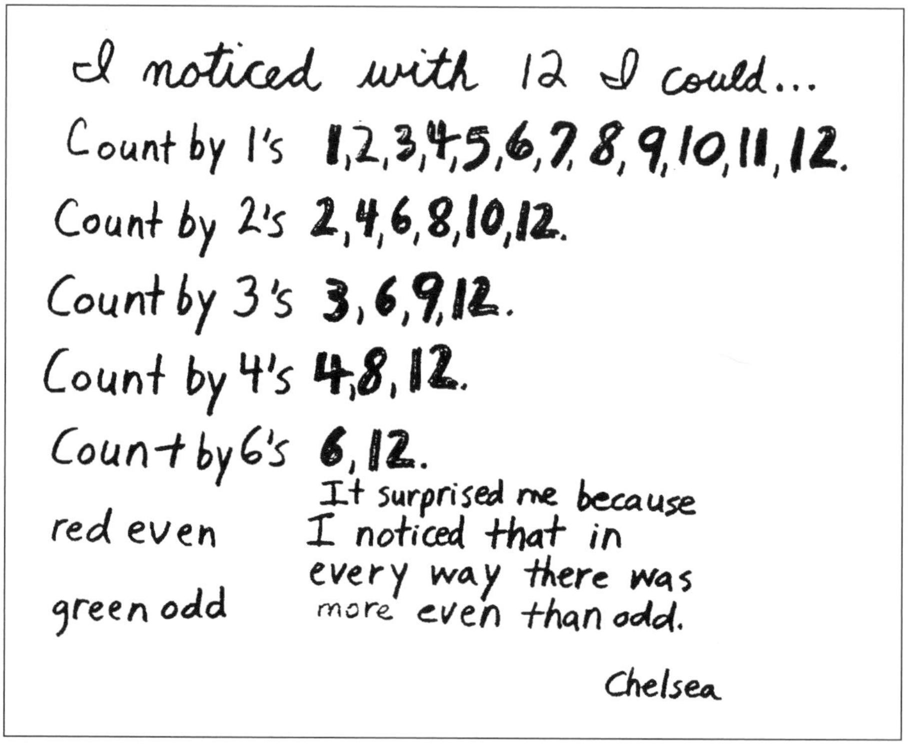

I noticed with 12 I could...
Count by 1's 1,2,3,4,5,6,7, 8, 9,10,11,12.
Count by 2's 2,4,6,8,10,12.
Count by 3's 3,6,9,12.
Count by 4's 4,8,12.
Count by 6's 6,12.

red even

green odd

It surprised me because I noticed that in every way there was more even than odd.

Chelsea

After listing the ways to count to 12, she traced each even number in red and each odd number in green. She was surprised at the proportion of even to odd numbers, and wrote, "It surprised me because I noticed that in every way there was more even than odd" (actually, there are the same number of even and odd numbers when counting by 2s and 3s but there are more even numbers altogether). Her use of color also showed that only even numbers appear when counting by 2s, 4s, and 8s, and that multiples of 4 and 6 are found within multiples of 2 (4 appears in the 4s line and 2s line; 6 appears in the 6s line and 2s line). Thus Chelsea not only highlighted some interesting patterns but also demonstrated how color can be an effective tool for displaying patterns that might lie hidden otherwise.

Joel and Whitney decided to record their surprise when they investigated ways to count to numbers beyond 12. Joel had expected smaller numbers to have fewer ways than larger numbers. He was surprised when his prediction did not hold true, and wrote, "It surprised me that thirteen only had two ways because thirteen is higher than nine and nine has more ways." Whitney encountered a similar surprise when she counted to nineteen: "I noticed that nineteen is such a big number but it only has two and sixteen has five." By reflecting upon these unexpected results in their journals, the children were compelled to revise their original hypotheses. Testing out additional numbers might then lead them to discover another reason to explain their findings. Again, it is this cycle of hypothesis-testing and reflecting that honors children as sense-makers and problem-solvers.

Colby envisioned the problem in another way by creating a metaphor. When David stopped by his desk, Colby remarked, "It's like a race. Twelve [counting by 12] gets there the fastest, and one gets there the slowest." Colby's idea stemmed from the journal prompt, "What does this pattern remind you of?" David encouraged Colby to draw a picture to show his idea (Figure 2-3).

Figure 2-3

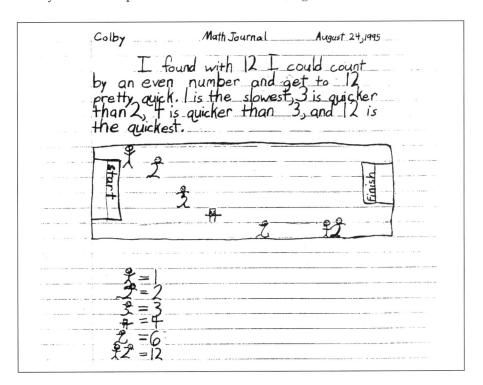

The figures, which embody the numbers they represent, are placed on the racing track according to how many hops are needed to reach twelve. Colby's unique interpretation captured the overall theme of the story of counting slowly and quickly by different intervals.

Reflecting on Our Decisions

In planning this experience, we had wanted to encourage a diversity of responses. We felt it was important to take the time to share various journals as a class so that the children could appreciate this diversity. We wanted to demonstrate that together our knowledge is greater than any one person's ideas alone. We also wanted to acknowledge the unique contribution of each student because we knew that some of the children had less confidence in math than others. We wanted all the children, not just the traditionally successful students, to be comfortable with taking risks. Sharing the ideas, as well as the inventiveness in displaying them (i.e., use of color or drawing), was one way to validate each person's contribution. Many children were delighted to show their journals to the class. Of course, the more shy children did not volunteer, but after we asked permission to show their work, many consented (on occasion, some children prefer to have their work photocopied on an overhead transparency without their names).

Together the class found some interesting relationships, and they appreciated their classmates for highlighting these different connections. Chelsea and Selita had used color to highlight their ideas. Colby's metaphorical drawing showed the total number of steps in sequential order, while Selita's bar graph emphasized the commutative relationship. Chelsea highlighted a pattern of odd and even numbers, and Joel and Whitney began to notice the attributes of prime and composite numbers. Maggie's idea of creating new counting patterns opened yet another avenue for exploration. What had begun with reading aloud a simple folk tale had led to a fund of ideas for future investigation, and a wealth of options for displaying and interpreting mathematical relationships. During the discussion, we teachers emphasized that using someone's idea for color, or extending a classmate's exploration of odd and even numbers, was not cheating; instead, the ideas of others are inspirations for new investigations. For example, when we showed Chelsea's journal entry, we commented, "We appreciate how Chelsea has shown how color can be a helpful way to find patterns. Next time other people might want to borrow Chelsea's strategy and see what they can discover by using color." It is also important to note that the class had developed more options for exploration than they could possibly follow. On later occasions, the class did explore the relationship between odd and even numbers as well as prime and composite numbers. No one, even Maggie, ever did continue to follow alternating patterns of counting. However, her invention was still an important contribution to the conversation. Just as writers benefit from entertaining multiple ideas for revision, so do mathematicians benefit from considering mathematical problems from various perspectives.

Using Children's Literature to Understand Large Numbers

Big numbers are difficult to understand, even for adults. By encouraging children to create models for these large numbers, and to use writing and talking as tools for understanding, teachers can help make these large numbers more accessible to children (Schwartz & Whitin, 1998). David Schwartz's popular books, *How Much is a Million* (1985) and *If You Made a Million* (1989) are wonderful tools in helping children to make sense of these large numbers. For example, he compares the amount of time it would take to count to one million (23 days nonstop) with the time to count to one billion (95 years). Such specific examples provide benchmarks for comparison, as well as a guide for understanding the exponential increase of these numbers. We found these books to be favorites of the fourth graders, and we have read each of them aloud on several occasions.

Connecting the Literature to Work with Base Ten Blocks

Throughout the year, we also used the base ten blocks to give the children a concrete model that illustrated the relationship between ones, tens, hundreds, and thousands. After reading *How Much is a Million* to the children, however, we began to wonder how we might connect the knowledge the children had about base ten blocks with the visual examples from Schwartz's book. We decided to link the two experiences by inviting the children to create base ten block models for numbers larger than one thousand.

A small group of children had formed a "Math Club" which met once a week before school. We chose to involve these children in the exploration first. We began by counting aloud together by hundreds as we built a thousand block out of 10 flats. After "nine hundred" some children chanted, "Ten hundred," while others chimed, "One thousand." We stopped to talk about the two ways to name numbers in the thousands, such as "twenty-five hundred" or "two thousand, five hundred." This discussion helped emphasize the language of large numbers and its role in conveying mathematical relationships. We then asked the group if they had enough blocks to build a structure containing one million centimeter cubes. After some discussion, they decided they might have about 10,000 units in the classroom collection, but surely not one million. We then challenged the children to build a structure that represented one million centimeter cubes.

We set aside another time for the actual building. However, before beginning the construction of this model, we reviewed with the children the relationship among the pieces (Figure 2-4).

Figure 2-4

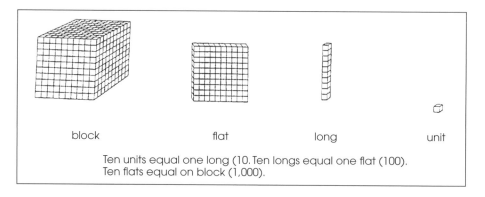

block   flat   long   unit

Ten units equal one long (10. Ten longs equal one flat (100).
Ten flats equal on block (1,000).

The children realized that the most efficient way to build a million-cube was to use their largest piece (the one-thousand block) as the unit of measure. However, since we only had a few of the one-thousand blocks, the children were not sure of how to proceed. After some discussion, they decided to represent 10 rows of 10 thousand-blocks by a 100 x 100 cm. square on the rug (Figure 2-5).

Figure 2-5
Photo Illustrating
One Million Centimeter
Cubes by Using
100 x 100 x 100
Centimeter Dimensions

The photograph shows how the children used wooden and paper flats to fill the entire square. The children then placed one of the thousand blocks in the corner of this square and found that they had represented one hundred one-thousand blocks for this first layer of the cube. Eric observed that our construction, "looks like a big flat. The thousand-block is like a unit." Building off this idea, Danny predicted that 1,000 of the thousand-blocks would make one million cubic centimeters because one thousand of the unit cubes made a thousand-block. Again counting together, we imagined layer upon layer of ten-100,000 pieces, "One hundred thousand, two hundred thousand, three hundred thousand . . . " until we reached, "Ten hundred thousand," or one million. They used a meter stick to demonstrate that the height of this million-cube was 100 cm. Satisfied with their accomplishments, the "Math Club" members presented their findings to the class later that morning. Having the opportunity to explain their reasoning to another audience helped them work through their understanding of large numbers once again.

At first the children (and adults) wanted to build a solid cube to represent 1,000,000. However, we soon realized that a structure that large would not fit through the door! Instead, we decided to make six faces of a hollow cube, which could easily be broken down and transported to other classrooms. Children could then assemble the cube by holding the six faces in place. In order to show how the million-cube was related to the base blocks the children covered each face with 100 paper flats, which they carefully colored in with bright crayons (Figure 2-6).

Figure 2-6
Photo of Children
Holding Six Faces of
Transportable
Million-Cube

Everyone wanted to share this collaborative creation with other children in the school. This enthusiasm led to the writing of a script for a "Traveling Million Show."

Sharing Discoveries outside Our Classroom

We spent a math period discussing how to explain our million structure to other groups of children. The fourth-graders realized that younger students would need to see the relationship among units, longs, flats, and a thousand-block to understand how the million-cube was constructed. Remembering how counting and assembling larger and larger pieces led to their own understanding, several children suggested that the younger children should count aloud by hundreds to a thousand, from thousands to one hundred thousand, and from hundred thousands to one million. Deidre suggested that relating the unit to a penny, the long to a dime, and the flat to a dollar would help as well. After this brainstorming session, Phyllis typed a sheet of directions labeled, "Million Show Script." All but five members of the class wanted to join a team to bring the "Million Show" to other classes. Phyllis posted a sign-up sheet on the teacher's message board, and soon teams of children took turns practicing and then enacting the "Million Show" to audiences throughout the school. Sharing their understanding of one million in this published form paved the way for the next challenge: representing one billion.

Devising a Model to Demonstrate One Billion

As a culminating project for the year, we decided to ask the children how we might construct a model that would be as large as one billion centimeter cubes. We asked each child to write and draw his or her solution to the problem for homework. We found that many students had indeed determined that a billion-cube would be equivalent to one thousand million-cubes, or a structure that was ten meters by ten meters by ten meters. Other children had not found the correct solution, but elements of their thinking were very sound. For example, Danielle wrote:

> If 1,000 thousand cubes equal 1,000,000, then 1,000,000 million cubes would equal a billion. What we could do is measure how tall and wide the million cube is and do that ten times, or we could do it 1,000,000 times. If we are not finished by the end of the year, then we could schedule a weekend to do the rest just for fun.

Danielle's solution of one million cubes was incorrect, but her suggestion of using a million-cube as a unit of measure was helpful.

We knew that sharing different perspectives aloud would enable some children to solidify their thinking while allowing others to revise and elaborate upon their original ideas. Deidre spoke next, suggesting that one million million cubes would make one billion, since one billion was such a big number. Tony followed by saying, "I think maybe a hundred might make it."

David repeated, "OK. A hundred. A hundred of those millions. What would 100 one-million blocks be?" All this talk about one million cubes supported Billy to propose another idea: "I think that we would need one thousand of the million cubes." It is likely that Billy used David's question to help him count by 100 millions. Although David's question, "What would 100 million cubes be?" was directed to Tony, it was Billy who used this information to describe his own understanding.

Brent approached the problem from a different angle by analyzing the number of zeros needed to represent one million and one billion. "I was going to say, because you have to make twelve zeros. . . . at first you have 9 zeros [thinking that one million had nine zeros], you have to make three more to make it."

Although Brent's actual number of zeros was inaccurate, his idea of thinking in terms of zeros helped other children. (Children might also investigate this pattern of zeros using the calculator). David answered, "OK now, actually there are six zeros for one million, and nine for one billion. So what would you think then?"

Rett was eager to contribute. "I wrote [last night for homework] that one thousand million cubes would make a billion. Now I saw that the zeros in one million plus one thousand [or plus the three zeros in one thousand], would equal nine, so it would be one billion if we had one thousand millions."

Chris, who had calculated one thousand million cubes, was also impressed by Rett's explanation. He said, "I was going to say that I thought it was a thousand million cubes, too. On my paper, I said a thousand meters, but I meant ten meters across. And now I'm really sure that it's a thousand. On my paper I said, 'I think it's a thousand million cubes because a thousand units make one of the thousand blocks, and a thousand blocks make a million, and so a thousand millions make a billion.' And now I know because on one, you add three zeros to make a thousand, and you add three more zeros for a million, so if you add three more zeros, it's a billion."

Although Chris had the correct solution, as well as a solid argument to justify his answer, he too benefited from the conversation. Rett's idea made Chris more sure of his own answer. Chris's understanding was deepened and broadened by this collaborative sharing of ideas.

Building the Model

We next turned to the problem of how we would build a model of a thousand million-cubes. Jenny suggested that we could use the length of a million-cube as a measuring stick and Danielle thought of a tape measure. She added that we might need a "ladder that stretches out" in order to measure the height, now that she had a more clear sense that this structure was going to be much higher than she had originally thought. The children wanted to start by using wood or cardboard to make one large face of the billion-cube. However, when we pointed out to the children that the height of this cube was going to be taller than the school (a two-story building), they realized that wood or cardboard was not going to be feasible. We suggested that they show the height using string that was tied to helium balloons. The children agreed to this idea. They were now ready to tackle the billion challenge.

On the appointed Billion Day, we assembled string, four tent stakes, two trundle wheels, and four large helium balloons. We also brought outside our six faces of the million-cube, a thousand-block, and a unit cube so that children could appreciate the proportionate difference among all these cubes. A parent volunteer worked with one group of children to tape the million-cube together and place it in the middle of the space we had designated as our building area. Next, they placed the thousand-block on top of the million-cube, and then the single centimeter unit on top of the thousand-block. This arrangement of successively larger cubes illustrated the exponential power of a base system, as each cube grew one thousand times larger each time (10^3, 10^6, 10^9). Other children measured ten-meter sides of our imagined cube. At each corner of this ten-meter square, the children drove a stake into the ground. They connected the stakes with string and then marked each string at one-meter intervals with ribbon. The bright red ribbon helped to emphasize how each side of this cube was composed of ten meters. Still other children cut ten-meter lengths of string to tie to the four balloons. To increase the drama of this final task, these children held the balloons while the group chanted a countdown. At the command, "Blast off!" the children released the balloons. However, instead of floating to their ten-meter height, they drooped to the ground. How disappointing! Even the adults had not been able to imagine that the weight of a ten-meter piece of string would be too heavy for each balloon to lift. The billion-cube was indeed larger than any of us had anticipated. Thinking quickly, we cut the strings of three of the balloons and tied all four to one string. With the extra lifting power, the one single string rose to its full ten-meter height and we all stared in awe at the enormity of our creation. The million-cube certainly looked small in comparison. Three zeros make a big difference. We left the structure outdoors so that other classes could observe our new discovery.

Reflecting upon the Model

When we returned to the classroom, we asked the children to write about the building experience, what they learned, and what they now wondered. We wanted to give each child the time to commit his or her concluding reflections on paper. The Standards emphasize regular opportunities for students to "reflect on and clarify their thinking about mathematical ideas and situations" (1989, p. 26). Their work demonstrated a wide range of personal response. Andrew, for example, connected the size of the billion-cube to the size of his own home to explain his new understanding of large numbers:

> When I came to school at the beginning of the year I never thought we would make a million or a billion. We showed a billion by making a block ten meters long on each side and raised balloons ten meters high. I learned that a billion is huge. It's almost as big as my house and as wide.

Eric, like Andrew, used familiar surroundings to think about what he had learned. He predicted that one trillion cubes would be bigger than the soccer field. Other children's reflections about one trillion were more numerical in nature. William drew upon his work with the idea of trading (regrouping) base ten blocks to write:

> 1. We showed one billion by getting balloons to show how tall one billion would be and yarn to show the width across.
> 2. I learned that each number like one thousand, one million, and billions, all trade after one thousand of that number.
> 3. I wonder how big one trillion is? Would it be one thousand billions because after one thousand millions and one thousand billions they all go to the next largest number like from one thousand to one million.

Rhiannon included a picture with her writing (Figure 2-7). Throughout the year, she had regularly sketched in her math journal; drawing was an important tool for her to express her thinking. She carefully included details, such as the tied yarn pieces that divided the long sides into 10 one-meter segments, and the shapes of the four helium balloons. She described the process of constructing the billion-cube, concluding with, "I learned how big a trillion is because it is a thousand billions." Chris decided that the new dimensions would be one hundred meters by one hundred meters, by one hundred meters (Figure 2-8).

Other children wrote about the comparative size of the million and billion models. Jenny wrote (Figure 2-9):

> I learned that ten meters was big with a capital B. I know because I was on strings. But I just thought that was big. When we tied the balloons and let them up. WOW! I also looked down, and when I saw a tiny square that was a million, I thought it was big, but next to

Figure 2-7

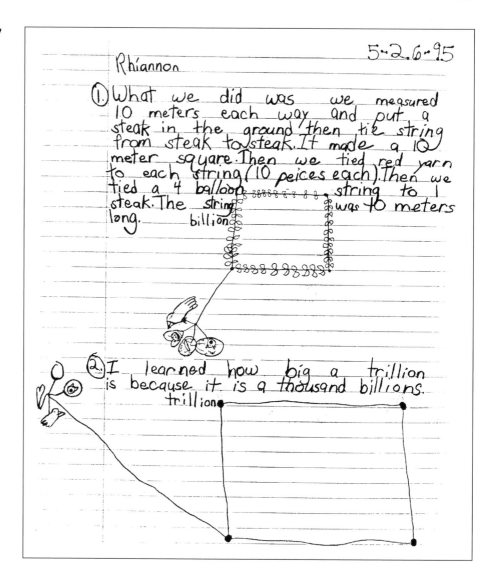

a billion it's nothing. When I read *How Much is a Million* and it said a billion kids could all go on shoulders and they'd go into space, well, I sort of didn't believe it, but now I would. I wonder how big a trillion would be. Maybe it would be as tall as that tree in that famous forest. I think it was something like redwood or something like that.

Jenny's reflection demonstrates the importance of building models to show the difference between one million and one billion. At the beginning of the year, the children saw both these numbers as simply "big numbers." However, by talking about the relationship

Figure 2-8

Figure 2-9

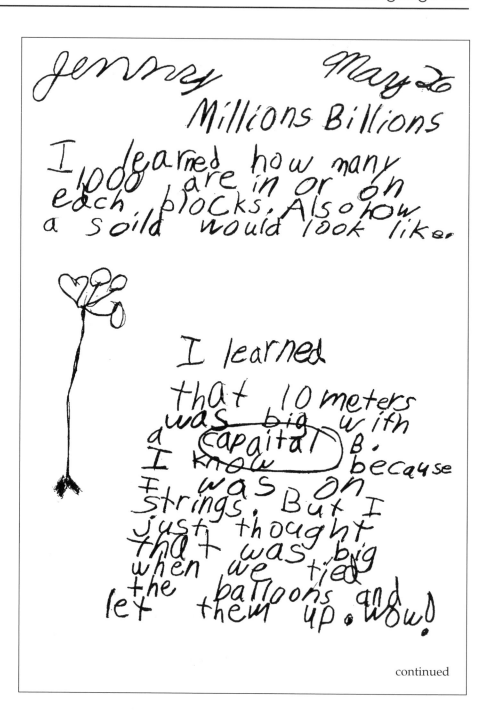

Jenny   May 26
          Millions Billions
I 1000 learned how many
each are in or on
each blocks. Also how
a soild would look like

I learned
that 10 meters
was big with
a (capaital) B.
I know because
I was on
strings. But I
just thought
that was big
when we tied
the balloons and
let them up. Wow!

continued

Figure 2-9 continued

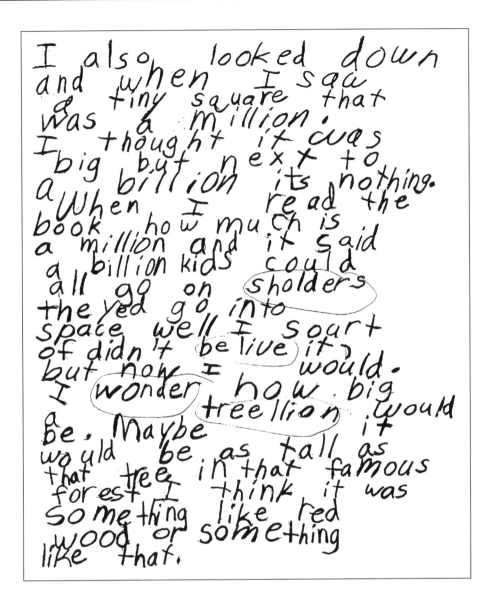

I also looked down and when I saw a tiny square that was a million. I thought it was big but next to a billion its nothing. When I read the book how much is a million and it said a billion kids could all go on sholders theyed go into space well I soart of didn't belive it but now I would. I wonder how big treellion it would be. Maybe it would be as tall as that tree in that famous forest I think it was something like red wood or something like that.

between these large numbers, creating a model for each one, and then taking the time to reflect upon this building experience, Jenny and her classmates had developed a deeper understanding for the magnitude of large numbers.

Tony learned another important lesson. He wrote: "I learned that it takes team work to build something big, and you can't do it by yourself." To us, Tony's remark underscored the value not only of working together to build the physical model, but also the benefit of sharing questions and ideas to strengthen our collective mathematical understanding. Developing a solid base of mathematical understanding is always "something big"; by talking, writing, planning and building as a community, we go farther together than any of us could go alone.

Reflecting on Our Decisions

This investigation into large numbers highlighted the value of talk. The students used talk as a tool for explaining and exploring their mathematical understanding. For instance, counting aloud by one hundreds helped them to see the equivalence of "ten hundred" and "one thousand"; counting aloud by one hundred-thousands helped show the equivalence of "ten hundred-thousands and "one million." In fact, this talking aloud was such an effective strategy that they decided to invite their younger audiences to do this same kind of pattern counting during their "Traveling Million Show." This show was another important learning experience because it gave the students an opportunity to reshape and publish their understanding for a new audience. Students need regular opportunities to publish mathematical texts throughout the year. The value of exploratory talk was demonstrated when the children shared their rough-draft thinking of how large one billion was. Brent's focus on the number of zeros helped Rett and Chris solidify their own understanding of how large this number really was. It was in the ways that talk played an essential role in deepening students' understanding of place value and large numbers.

This long-term project also illustrates the power of writing and drawing as tools for reflection. Some children, like Andrew, who compared the size of the billion-cube to his house, grew by connecting school and home experiences. Others, like Chris and William, used writing as an analytical tool to describe mathematical relationships. Rhiannon was one of the children who often expressed her thinking through drawing. Her reflective journal includes details of the model she built as well as speculation about possible extensions. Using writing and drawing as tools for reflection enables children to make their thinking visible in personally meaningful ways.

Using Children's Literature to Understand Mathematical Vocabulary

Children's literature can also be an avenue for students to explore the meaning of mathematical vocabulary. We read the story *One Hundred Hungry Ants* (Pinczes, 1993) as a way to introduce prime and composite numbers to children. This is a story in verse that describes a group of ants that arrange and rearrange themselves in various arrays (2 x 50, 4 x 25, and so on).

Exploring the Ideas in the Story

After enjoying the story, we gave the children a pile of one-inch tiles and asked them to find all the possible ways to arrange a given number of them into rectangles. For example, with twelve tiles the children could build a 1 x 12 going horizontally, a 12 x 1 vertically, 3 x 4, 4 x 3, 6 x 2, and 2 x 6. The children also noticed that some numbers, such as 5, 7, 13, could be arranged in only two ways: one long row and one long column. After collecting a list of "numbers that only have two ways" (which in math terminology are called "primes"), and "numbers that have more than two ways," (in math terminology, "composites"), we asked the children to create names for these special kinds of numbers based on what the tile arrangements reminded them of. After a brainstorming session, the children wrote about their ideas. Creating these names enabled the children to demonstrate an important aspect of the Standards: "relating their everyday language to mathematical language and symbols" (1989, p. 26).

The children's names for prime numbers were metaphors that reflected images of narrow objects or designs. William, for example, wrote, "I chose lane numbers (for primes) because they look like lanes on a highway." He also described them as "skinny numbers because they look like they are very skinny." The children created a variety of associations for composite numbers: "King Kong numbers because King Kong is big and the numbers are big" (meaning numbers that have more than two factors), "checker numbers because they look like a checkerboard"; and "greedy numbers because the bigger numbers look like they ate more than the others." Rhiannon explained, "I like sidewalks and ladders because the tall ones (a single column of tiles) look like ladders, and the short ones look like a sidewalk" (Figure 2-10). She contrasted these thin arrangements with a name for composite numbers: "6, 8, 10, 12, 14, and 16 are 'variety numbers' because there is a variety" (that is, a variety of ways to construct rectangles of those numbers of tiles). All of these students emphasized the physical appearance of the arrays. However, Rett called primes, "kin numbers" because "they can only go two ways and they look like they're related." Rett's comment underscored the commutative property of multiplication (i.e. 1 x 7 is the same as 7 x 1). Two facts, such as 1 x 5 and 5 x 1, can be related just as relatives can be related. Building off the idea of relatives, Amanda called prime numbers, "twins" because there were only two possible arrangements. She then extended the idea of twins by creating a new association: "I picked twins because they look the same, but one likes to look up, and one likes to look across (Figure 2-11). Amanda's imaginative drawing helped emphasize the concept of congruence. The pair of eyes shows that the two rectangles, like identical twins, are really the same; they only have a different horizontal or vertical

Figure 2-10

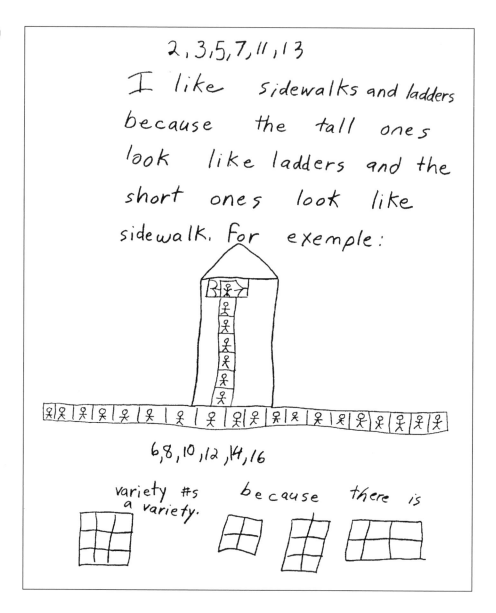

2, 3, 5, 7, 11, 13
I like sidewalks and ladders because the tall ones look like ladders and the short ones look like sidewalk. For exemple:

6, 8, 10, 12, 14, 16

variety #s a variety. because there is

orientation. Her sketch demonstrates the potential of expressing mathematical ideas through the medium of drawing.

Nicholas, too, drew upon the physical appearance of the tiles by calling prime numbers "T numbers" because the two arrays could be placed in a "t" shape. However, it was his name for composite numbers that drew our attention. He called composite numbers "monster numbers, because it (they) scare you away." David asked Nicholas why composite numbers were scary. He explained

Figure 2-11

that prime numbers were "easy" because the factors could be listed quickly. Composites, on the other hand, took "a lot of work" to describe because of the larger number of possible factors. David challenged Nicholas to show his idea for "a lot of work" in a new way. Nicholas took the challenge, ironically causing him to do more work, and created Figure 2-12! His graph contrasts prime numbers such as 0, 1, 2, 3, 7 as "easy," while 4, and 6 require work. Highest on the chart is 24, which according to Nicholas was "super lot of work." Nicholas extended the idea of naming a number metaphorically by inventing a picture that compared the first 24 counting numbers. Nicholas's experience illustrated an important benefit of children's inventing their own mathematical vocabulary: By inviting the children to generate images created from personal experiences, we celebrated their individual aptitudes and perspectives. Nicholas, like Amanda, used a visual image to convey his ideas. Amanda's sketch of eyes captured a feeling of movement, while Nicholas's reflected a more analytical stance.

Soon after this experience, we told the children about the traditional terms, prime, and composite. We talked as a class about their etymologies and the uses of these words in other contexts. For example, we explained that the root for "factor" is the same as "factory" and "manufacture." The meanings for all three words are linked because they all deal with making products. The connotations of "prime time" or "prime cut" were similar to the descriptions that the children had created, emphasizing being unique or first. The children were beginning to appreciate that even conventional mathematical terms have metaphorical roots. Encouraging metaphorical images for mathematical ideas restores the story that has led to conventional terminology.

Figure 2-12

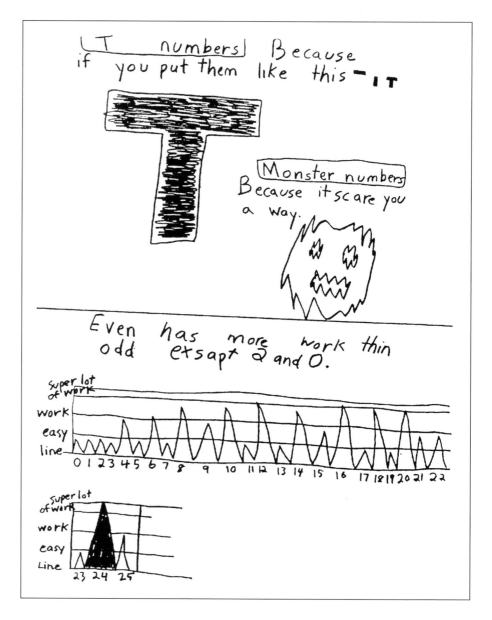

We have also found that metaphorical thinking can connect class experiences across traditional subject lines. An experience with children the following year clearly demonstrated this idea to us. Again, we asked the children to create metaphorical descriptions for prime and composite numbers. This particular class had been fascinated with population density and the size of various cities as they studied the regions of the United States in social studies. They had contrasted the Mid-Atlantic region, which has a very small land area but a high population density, with the Mountain West, which has the opposite characteristics. Ryan suggested "Mountain West numbers" for primes to reflect its sparse population and "Mid-Atlantic numbers" for composites because of its dense population and number of cities over 1,000,000. It is interesting that this metaphor also connected two separate mathematical ideas, density (ratio), and prime and composite numbers. Creating metaphors in mathematics opens doors for these intriguing connections.

Reflecting on Our Decisions

Creating mathematical metaphors supports children to be risk-takers. No metaphor that the children suggested was "wrong"; rather, each highlighted a different attribute of the numbers. For instance, some metaphors emphasized the shape of the rectangles (skinny, King Kong); others related to the way the rectangles were oriented in space (sidewalks and ladders); and still others accentuated the range of factors (scary, greedy, and variety numbers). This variety of images reflected the unique talents and interests of the group's members. It is through differences that we can uplift the individual voices of our students. As Eisner states (1991, p. 16): "Variance, not homogeneity, is what counts in schooling." We must design the environments and plan the invitations that make that variance possible.

Metaphors also gave the class a rich reservoir of images for describing the properties of these numbers. For this reason we have often postponed the use of conventional mathematical terms until students have had the opportunity to describe that concept in their own way first. Mathematics textbooks often operate in just the reverse order: students are introduced to the proper vocabulary first before being allowed to use that concept themselves. We think that sequence of instruction is putting the cart before the horse. It is only in using a concept that learners can develop an appreciation for what it looks like and what it can do; by labeling mathematical ideas from the start we sometimes curtail children's own powers of analysis and description (Borasi, 1992). However, by asking, "What does this mathematical pattern, or idea, remind you of?" we invite students to create a pool of mathematical associations. Naming mathematical ideas they encounter enables learners to retain responsibility for their definition and development. This is not to say that we do not introduce children to the proper mathematical terms. We certainly do, but only after the children have described these ideas in their own way first. As Joan Countryman says, "Definitions alone rarely throw much light on the ideas they represent" (1992, p. 55). When the focus is exclusively on the standard terminology, learners sometimes hide behind the labels. For those children who might know some of the proper terms at the beginning of an investigation, we respond to their comments by seeking further description: "Tell us what you mean by a prime number" or "What do you find interesting about composite numbers?" In this way children can speak for themselves, and not let these conventional labels do the talking for them.

Conclusion

Children's literature can help students value the process, honor surprise, acknowledge the contributions of others, and grow through reflection. Students value the process when they are given the time to work through their own problems, such as how to represent one million, or how to represent patterns in factors. Students honor surprise when they are encouraged to make those surprises public, such as Whitney and Joel wondering why 13 has fewer factors than 9. Students appreciate the contributions of others by acknowledging a wide range of responses, such as Colby's metaphor, Chelsea's color pattern, and Nicholas's picture for number factors. Lastly, children view reflection as an important part of their own growth, such as Jenny's comparison of one million and one billion. It is in these ways that the strategic use of children's literature can open the potential for much writing and talking about mathematical ideas. It is through stories that students can stake out their own personal identities as well as contribute to the collective pool of mathematical understanding.

Understanding Algorithms from the Inside Out

At the beginning of Chapter 1 we introduced you to a disempowered learner named Justin, a second grader who saw mathematics as right answers only. In this chapter, we want to examine the conditions under which learners can still get right answers—but with understanding and a sense of ownership. We have come to realize that right answers are not synonymous with understanding; in fact, right answers sometimes convey a veneer of accomplishment on minds that are not thinking for themselves (Hiebert, 1997). On the other hand, sometimes-wrong answers can mask quite sophisticated mathematical thinking (such as Gaye's solution for 184 divided by 2 in Chapter 1). In either case, we now want to look at how writing and talking can be tools for peeling back that veneer of competence and allowing children to think and reason for themselves.

If we view children as sense-makers, then even algorithms (procedures for performing calculations) can be grounds for discovery and surprise (Madell, 1985; Kamii, Lewis, & Livingston, 1993; Cochran, Barson, & Davis, 1970). We have already discussed a few brief examples in Chapter 1 of how personal inventiveness and reflection can be avenues for exploring the meaning of algorithms. In this chapter, we want to look at the area of computation more closely and examine how diversity, surprise, and reflection can still be nurtured. Even in the area of computation, which traditionally has been taught in a rote way, it is important to build a classroom community that recognizes the thinking of others. For instance, teachers can make public a variety of responses, such as personal descriptions, drawings, and narratives. The Standards stress the importance of children having numerous opportunities to "relate physical materials, pictures, and diagrams to mathematical ideas. . . . The use of concrete materials is particularly appropriate because they give the children an initial basis for conversation" (1989, pp. 26–27). There can be surprises in computational problems as well if children are encouraged to look closely and describe what they find interesting. Reflection about the process is also possible when children are asked to predict their answers first; these predictions often lead to revisions in thinking, a critical dimension of independent, empowered learners. Reflection can also be promoted by inviting children to analyze common computational miscues and argue the logic behind those responses; another strategy is for children to examine the thinking of their peers, try to make sense of it themselves, and then compare it to what they have tried. Lastly, having children create their own computational problems gives them an audience for their writing as well as a window into their mathematical thinking. These are the various strategies we will highlight in this chapter. As in the previous chapters we want to draw out children's sense-making efforts, and with that their personal experiences and individual voices (Lampert, 1990; Whitin & Whitin, 1998). Fostering this exploratory stance in computation begins with the first experiences that we provide children.

Exploring Computation Informally through Games

It's been our experience that in any classroom children reflect their past instructional history. Some children come with a solid foundation of place value and a flexibility in using various mental math strategies. Others, however, solve problems using a set of procedures, but often do not understand the conceptual principles behind those procedures. For this reason we find that using base ten block manipulatives to be a helpful tool for addressing this range of strengths and needs. First we give students some opportunity to discover the relationships among the pieces, i.e., ten units are equivalent to a "long," ten longs fit completely on top of a "flat," and ten flats can be built into the form of a "block" (thousand). Next, we play informal games such as the Show Me Game:

> *Teacher:* On your desk, show me 52. How do you know your blocks show 52?
>
> *Student:* Five longs equal 50, and there are two units, so it makes 52.

Variations include, "Show me 10 more than 68; show me 20 less than 83," and so forth. At this point, we are working on familiarity with the blocks, place value, and simple mental math. Our question, "Why does that make sense . . . ?" stresses the thinking behind the correct answer. (For additional warm-up activities with base ten blocks, see Appendix 1; for instructions to make inexpensive paper models, see Appendix 2).

Once students are familiar with the base ten blocks, we spend a day or two playing the Trading Game. Games provide a supportive context for students to devise mental computation strategies for efficient and flexible use. We have also found that games give a relaxed and informal atmosphere to computation, and that reflecting upon game strategies can lead to fruitful writing and talking about algorithms. In the Trading Game students take turns rolling a number cube (die) and placing the corresponding number of units on a playing board labeled from right to left: units, longs, flats. When one of the partners accumulates 10 units, he or she trades them for a long. The game continues until one player reaches a flat (100). We give some choices for rules. For example, the team of players can decide if they want to end by rolling the exact sum of 100, or if they will accept a final play that results in a total of 100 or greater. They also can choose to compete (each player having a separate board), or to work as a team together to make one flat. After a demonstration game on the overhead, the children try a warm-up game. We adults circulate around the room, noticing which children are able to make a ten without counting each individual unit. For example, if a child has 8 on the board and rolls a 5, does she gather another 5 from the 8 to make a ten, and leave 3; or does she count out 5 new units, and then go back to resume counting "6, 7, 8, 9, 10" from the 8 units on the board? In the latter case, the student does not rename 8 as 5 + 3 to make the adding more efficient. She needs to count each unit separately. This informal assessment helps us plan in many ways. We may decide to put students of different abilities together the next day; we may choose to talk about strategies with one team quietly between games, or we may spend time reviewing strategies for mental math with the whole group.

Sharing Observations about the Trading Game

After a warm-up game or two, we stop to discuss what the students have noticed or what they have found interesting so far. We purposely use "notice," and "find interesting" orally because these words are used in the journal prompts. We make brief notes on the board about their observations. Both the talking and the collective list on the board prepare the children for the journal writing that will come later. We also might say, "I noticed that Carla, Nia, and some others were able to predict when they would make a long without counting each block. Can one or two of you tell us about what was going on in your mind as you made your prediction?" We want the children to practice analyzing mental math strategies, putting them into words, and making them public. After oral sharing, we tell the children to pay close attention to their own observations and strategies during the next game in order to be able to write about their thinking in their journals.

A sampling of journal responses from early one September shows a diversity of ideas. Jacqui chose to write about her team's decision to end the game with an exact roll for 100. She drew 9 longs and 8 units, and wrote, "I discovered that if you play the hard way it is difficult because if you have 98, you have to roll a 2 or 1. That was the mess I was in, but I rolled a two and won." Jacqui realized that only 2 out of the 6 possibilities would enable her to put a piece on her board, and that narrow range of options made her game difficult.

Casey and Jake analyzed another aspect of the game. During our informal sharing time, many children had talked about how fast or slow their game progressed. We suggested that some people might want to keep track of how many rolls it took them to get to 100. A conversation began at one table when Casey discovered that it took her 27 rolls to get to 100. Phyllis extended this observation by asking: "I wonder what is the fewest number of rolls you need to get to 100? Or the most?" Jake took the challenge, worked for awhile, and wrote in his journal: "I discovered that it took at least 17 rolls to get 100. 6 x 17 = 102." One of our goals at this point of the year was to demonstrate to children that writing and keeping records can preserve thinking and generate interesting new discoveries. Jake was comfortable with mental addition, but writing and talking about the game in open-ended ways gave him an opportunity to extend his thinking.

Casey also wrote about the advantage of using mental math strategies to speed up her game. She wrote, "My strategy was to keep on adding blocks and regrouping and rolling as fast as I could. Like if I had 8 and I rolled a 5, I knew I would have to regroup because I had to get at least 2 or more, and I got 5." Casey knew that by thinking ahead and mentally calculating the minimum roll required for an exchange, her game became more efficient. Her journal served as a record of this strategic thinking. Other children interpreted the word *strategy* more broadly, writing comments such as, "My strategy was to drop the dice on the desk and hope for a six." Through class discussions and journal sharing, we would work to define the word *strategy* in a more mathematical sense by stressing thoughtful planning rather than wishful thinking.

More Formal Work with Algorithms

As children work more formally with computation, we want to continue to emphasize strategic thinking and reasoning, as well as promote a personal style of expression. Our teaching continues to include these three important strategies: (1) choose our language carefully (i.e. continue to use words such as "predict," "notice," "strategy," "why does that make sense," and so forth), (2) provide time for the oral rehearsal of ideas through group brainstorming, and (3) highlight a diversity of journal responses to build a collective fund of ideas. These three strategies value the social nature of learning and support a risk-taking attitude that continues to generate new ideas.

Supporting the Strategy of Predicting

The Trading Game leads naturally to work with addition. One way to begin to write about addition is to have each partner build one addend of a problem. As they study the two boards, we ask them to predict what will happen when the two collections are combined. A simple beginning problem might be: "Partner #1 build 45 on your board. Partner #2 build 78. Look at your two collections and predict what will happen when you combine them." Children typically offer observations such as these:

- You will need to trade for a flat.
- You will need to trade units for a long.
- The answer will have three digits.

Our response to each of their comments continues to be, "How do you know?" Defending their answers, even for simple problems, paves the way to writing for understanding. Of course, some children are eager to give the exact answer right away, but at this point, we want to emphasize the range of predictions we can make. Predicting can give children more time to analyze the whole problem as well as support them to make reasonable estimates. For example, Megan focused her prediction on the need for exchanging in the problem 68 + 75: "I notice that I will have to do some trading. I will have to trade in ten longs for a flat and ten units for a long." She mentions the need to exchange the tens first. This method of moving from left to right is quite common with students who are given the freedom to choose which strategy makes most sense to them (Kamii, Lewis, & Livingston, 1993).

Nia envisioned the problem 111 + 389 and then recorded her prediction in her journal.

There are 4 flats, 9 longs, and 10 units. If you add them together, I think you will have to do some trading because if you add the units together you will get 10, so you could add that to the longs and then you will only have flats because all the longs and units have been traded to a flat. You will have 5 flats and you get 500.

By taking time to study the blocks and make predictions, Nia calculated the total without using the traditional paper and pencil algorithm. The question, "What do you see is going to happen in this problem?" can lead to this kind of proficiency in mental mathematics.

Predicting is especially helpful with subtraction problems that involve regrouping. For instance, when Lori was solving the problem 500 − 368, she wrote:

$$
\begin{array}{r}
9 \\
4 \ \cancel{10} \ 10 \\
\cancel{5} \ \cancel{0} \ \cancel{0} \\
-3 \ 6 \ 8 \\
\hline
1 \ 3 \ 2
\end{array}
\qquad
\begin{array}{r}
132 \\
+368 \\
\hline
500
\end{array}
$$

What I right off know is that there are two zeros on the top number, and we will immediately go to the 5 and our answer will be less than 200 and greater than 100.

I was right. The answer is lower than 200 and more than 100. This subtraction problem is sort of like helping each number out so that it can subtract a number to get an answer.

Although we want children to predict the kind of exchanging they see in a problem, we do not want to limit what they see. We have found that by asking, "What do you notice?" and "What do you find interesting?" along with "What do you predict?", we leave room for open-ended possibilities. In the simple problem, 105 + 120, Selita realized that she would not need to exchange. However, she continued to write, "If we had five more units, we could have traded." She was used to looking for exchanging and envisioned a way the problem could be modified to make that exchanging necessary. On another occasion, Jeremy incorporated a personal mathematical interest when he solved the problem 310 – 185. He was always intrigued with odd and even numbers, and his journal reflected that interest.

$$
\begin{array}{r}
2 \ 10 \ 10 \\
\cancel{3} \ \cancel{1} \ 0 \\
-1 \ 8 \ 5 \\
\hline
1 \ 2 \ 5
\end{array}
$$

In my head I know that two of my flats are gone because it says to take one flat away, and I have one long, but I need ten longs. Then I have to take eight longs away, so I have two longs left. In my head I know that my number is going to be odd because a half of ten is five.

Both of these children's journals were valuable to share with the class. Selita's writing demonstrated that predicting can also entail imagining alternative problems. We used Jeremy's observation to encourage the class to investigate predictable patterns of odd and even numbers as they appeared in other operations.

Learning to Value Revision

Reflecting on their predictions can lead children to make revisions in their thinking. *Revise* is another word we have found to be helpful in nurturing positive mathematical attitudes. Many children are accustomed to the word *fix* when they change their minds about a mathematical problem. However, *fix* gives a connotation of a right/

wrong end product. We wanted a more positive alternative that highlighted the sense-making process, so we borrowed "revise" from the realm of writing. Authors celebrate revision as a way to make their writing better or more refined. Thoughtful revision is a sign of learning and of expertise. We now use the term from the first day of school. For example, in the problem 48 + 22, a student might say "Sixty . . . I mean, 70." We respond, "You just showed some excellent thinking by revising your answer. What helped you decide to revise your thinking?" As children become accustomed to using the idea of revision orally, they are ready to extend it to their writing.

An experience with a missing addend problem gave us the opportunity to discuss the importance of revising one's thinking as well as highlight the value of writing itself. We gave the problem 12 + ? = 100 and asked the children to predict, solve, and write about their strategies and discoveries. While they were working, Matt told David how he had changed his mind while solving the problem. David noticed that Matt had not included any information about this revision in his journal, and he urged him to write down what he had just said. We have found the suggestion, "That sounds like a really important idea to include in your journal. Write down just what you said," to be a helpful way to support children as they write. In this case, Matt added to his journal, "First I put 9 tens, but I knew that you could trade the units for another ten. And that is why I changed the 9 to a 8." Later we invited Matt to read his journal to the class and then asked the children why it was useful for Matt to write about his revision. Here is a portion of their discussion:

> *Jacqui:* He won't remember what he said (if he didn't write it down). It tells us what he did.

> *Carla:* I think it was a good idea because it shows how he was thinking.

> *Danny:* Well, mine is sort of like Carla's. I like to look back and see how . . . the history of that person's thinking, and how hard that problem used to be to them, and now it's like the easiest thing on earth. It showed that he matured a lot. You can mature very fast.

> *Jake:* I think it was a good idea to put that because you would know that at first it was hard for him, because at first he didn't know he had to trade to make a ten, and then make another ten to make a hundred. He would know that he had just a little bit of trouble and then it was easy for him.

> *Ryan:* I thought it was good because first he said 98, and then I thought he was revising his thinking. . . .he thought he was doing it very well, but at the end he did it a lot better, when he resolved [revised] his thinking.

Ashley: I think it was good that he had the 9, and then the 8, because he thought it was 98, but then he used his head and he wanted to go over it again to make sure that it was the right answer. And then he changed it and I think that was very smart.

It was important to take the time to reflect upon this simple journal entry. First, the children needed the opportunity to describe the value of writing in their own words. In this brief discussion, the children listed several benefits of writing about computation: it records our thinking for our own use or for communicating with others; it gives us a record of our growth as learners; it shows our self-reliance to revise on our own; and it reveals the thinking behind the numbers. Further, by highlighting a revised answer for discussion, we boosted the confidence of those children who did not have the "right" answer on the first try. We wanted to instill in them a sense of pride in thinking and rethinking for themselves. In this way the children could see the journals as records of thoughtfulness and sense making. Finally, Matt's experience provided us another opportunity to have children give each other appreciations. In these ways we work to build a safe community of mathematical thinkers who are willing to take risks and revise their thinking.

Developing a Personal Style

Just as we want children to value writing as a record of growth and achievement, we also want them to appreciate mathematical writing as a personal form of expression. We want children to find that by sharing one another's gifts and talents, the class as a whole is enriched. In Chapter 2, we celebrated a diversity of responses to literature. At the beginning of the year it is equally important to nurture their unique voices as they write and draw about computation. When we review journals, we make notes about the work of different children. We often ask those children to read their work aloud, and sometimes we make overhead transparencies of children's work to share. The students compliment one another on writing and drawing strategies that are clear, informative, and reflect a personal style. We have noticed that some shy children, many of whom are girls, rarely raise their hands for class discussions. We have found that by asking to share their journal entries (even without revealing their names), we have helped them develop confidence. Over time, many of these quiet students begin to contribute to class conversations. We want to make every child feel valued in the classroom. Making journals public regularly has been one of the most successful strategies we know to achieve this goal.

Some children develop a systematic way to show their work. Joshua invented a format for his writing by dividing and labeling his work with three sections: *Predict, Solve,* and *Write.* Here is a sample of his work:

```
      9
   41010
    500         132
   −368        +368
    132         500
```

Predict: I predict that I will have 400 (one flat traded). I'm probably going to trade a hundred in for some longs and some units.
Solve: I have just traded, and I have 10 units and 9 longs. (I don't have ten longs because I traded it in for some units). I also have 4 hundred.

Write: I have just subtracted. I have two units. There is three longs left now. There is one hundred now left.

We could have required the children to follow a prescribed format for their writing. Instead, we prefer giving this responsibility to the children. We then highlight a variety of these organizational tools and have the children express appreciations about the benefits of each. Then they have a wide range of styles to choose from, and each author feels recognized.

Other children find their writing voices through humor. Kyle, for example, added dialogue bubbles by his diagrams of blocks that needed regrouping, such as a single unit that asks, "Hey, can I borrow 10?" The long answers, "Sure." Justin used his journal to talk to himself in an amusing way. For the problem 174 − 82 = 92, he wrote:

```
   174
   −82
    92
```

1. I took 4 units and took away two units, so I have 2 units.
2. And I knew that 7 − 8 = Wait a second. I have to take the flat away so I would have 1 long, so 17 − 8 = 9. So my answer is 92 (easy).

Maggie's conversation with herself shows both humor and an honest admission of the frustration students feel when a problem requires a lot of "work."

```
    5 15
    265
   −138
    127
```

I knew that I was going to have to borrow a long. I said 8 can't go into 5, so I am going to have to take away a long. So I took a long and I put 10 units down and then I took away 8 and that = 7. So now I have to move to the tens. What happened? I only have 5 longs left. Oh, I forgot. I had to borrow one of the longs. So now it says I have to take 3 away. Gosh, I'm getting mad. I have to take 3 away. Well, I guess I have to do it. So I took 1,2,3 away and I only have 2 left. Well, let's go to the hundreds. I have to take 1 away, but I only have 2 so that would leave me with 1.

Cortney developed a more serious style of talking to herself on paper. She would begin each explanation with, "What did you do? HMMM. . . I see!!" The "HMMM" signified her thoughtful stance as she reviewed her thinking for a problem.

Often sharing these diverse kinds of responses gives more reluctant writers an idea of a format to follow. At other times whole classes adopt a word or phrase that a child used in a journal. For example, Chris invented his own way to describe regrouping when he explained the following problem:

$$\begin{array}{r} 67 \\ +38 \\ \hline 105 \end{array}$$

He wrote, "I added 7 and 8 and 6 and 3. 7 and 8 are being nice and giving 6 and 3 a 10. 6 and 3 are being nice and giving 0 one hundred." "Being nice" became a way for members of his class to make computational problems more like stories. Similarly, Lori influenced her class with her description of one block "helping out" another when exchanging was necessary. In a third class, Danny explained 324 divided by 4 by saying, "Three in the hundreds place can't support the 4." Other children adopted his term, "support," to describe the relationship between the divisor and the first digit of the dividend. Each of these classes developed their own language to describe the process of regrouping. Adopting unique class-generated vocabulary is another way to build a mathematical community while honoring individual voices.

Predicting and Sharing Our Thinking

Now that we have shared some initial experiences that have focused on prediction, revision, and personal expression, we will examine a range of written responses surrounding a single event. In this way, we can illustrate in more detail how individual voices strengthen a group's understanding.

We had been using base ten blocks with the children to show the process of division. For instance, when solving a problem such as 94 divided by 6, we would ask, "Look at your blocks, with nine longs and four units. If six people want to divide these pieces fairly among themselves, how much would each person get?" The children see that they could give each person one long, but then trade the remaining three longs for units. The children would then divide the 34 units among the six people, giving each person five, leaving a remainder of 4: 94 divided by 6 = 15 R4. We have found that encouraging children to predict some of this process can be helpful in developing good mental mathematics.

On this occasion, we asked the children to make predictions for 73 divided by 6. The children placed 7 longs (or tens) and 3 units on their board. We then asked, "Before we actually divide these blocks among six people, look closely at what you have right now and try to imagine what you see is going to happen in this problem. Write down these predictions in your journal." Next we asked the children to share what they had written. The diversity of their responses highlighted different aspects of the division process.

Tiff could foresee the problem from beginning to end and wrote a detailed description of the exchanging process: "I predict that you will have to trade a long in for units, and get 10 units and give them out and you will have a remainder of 1, and everybody gets 1 long and 2 units each. So 12 is your answer and a R 1." Megan saw the need for exchanging tens but justified it in this way: "I predict that you will have to trade one long in for 10 units because you don't have enough to go around twice." Her language revealed that she saw division as a process of successive subtractions, i.e. we can subtract one set of six tens but not two sets. Tony gave this same explanation but in a slightly different way: "I predict that we will have to trade a ten in for units because there are 7 tens, not 12 tens." Both these explanations complemented each other quite nicely: Megan contributed her visual description of "going around twice" and Tony calculated the exact number of tens necessary for this second cycle to occur.

Lauren and Stephanie described similar strategies as they used their number sense to estimate a reasonable answer. Lauren wrote: "I predict that there will be a remainder because 6 x 12 = 72 and 6 x 13 = 78." Her writing and mathematical equations helped to prove the conclusion that she drew. Stephanie wrote: "I predict that each person will get one long and three units. It has to be close to 10 but less than 20 because 20 x 6 is way too much." Both children tried to set boundaries for their answer. Lauren used her calculations to predict there would be a remainder, while Stephanie used her number sense to predict an answer closer to 10 than 20. It is this comparing and contrasting of strategies that highlights the rich potential of living in a collaborative community.

Jason and Alex were intrigued with the size of the remainder. Jason wrote: "You have to trade because if you don't your remainder will be too big." However, Alex was willing to consider a large remainder: "I predict that there will be 13 left over because the seventh 10 nobody could use them unless you break it up." Thus, Alex argued that 10 R 13 was one way to describe the answer. He also realized that further trading was only possible if the last 10 were broken up. His language of "breaking up a ten" provided the class with an interesting way to portray the exchanging process.

This range of responses highlights the power of children's descriptive language as well as their personal inventiveness. For instance, they gave numerous reasons for why exchanging in the problem, 73 divided by 6, was necessary: the remainder will be too big; there aren't enough tens to go around twice; and nobody can use the seventh ten unless it's broken up. Asking them to predict allowed for personal reflection about their problem-solving strategies, such as Stephanie's argument for why the answer would be closer to 10 than 20.

Predicting Leads to New Directions

However, other journal entries opened up new doors to investigate. Writing gave several children the opportunity to generate theories to explain what they saw happening. Once again, writing became a tool for discovering new thoughts and proposing new relationships. Lori and Jamie were intrigued with odd and even numbers as they viewed this problem. Lori suggested that the reason there was going to be a remainder was that 73 was composed of an odd number of longs and an odd number of units. Jamie wrote: "I predict that you will have to trade in some longs because 73 is an odd number. . . . Maybe even numbers [like the divisor of 6] can't go into odd numbers [like the dividend of 73]." Jamie's question was explored later when the children looked at factors of numbers and found that some odd numbers could "go into" even numbers (6 divided by 3 = 2) without a remainder, but no even number could "go into" an odd number without a remainder. Thus, Jamie and Lori highlighted a new dimension for the class to consider.

James pointed to another new direction by inquiring about the remainder: "I found that everyone gets 12, but there is 1 remainder. So what are you supposed to do with the extra unit?" When we raised this issue with the class we discussed the possibility of slicing the cube into sixths. Stephanie wondered how a different shape, like a circle, could be sliced into sixths, and then exclaimed, "Oh yeah, like a pizza." Thus, James's question raised the problem of partitioning volumes and areas into equal parts. We returned to this issue later in the year when we discussed fractions and decimals. We have found that children make these connections across mathematical concepts when they are given the opportunity to take risks; these risks include the freedom to raise questions, propose theories, and offer alternative explanations. In this way, making unexpected connections will come to be an expected norm of classroom life.

Responding Together through Class Response Sheets

Another way to promote class discussions about these various strategies is to create class response sheets (Figure 3-1). Occasionally we copy several children's journal entries on a single sheet of paper and photocopy them for the class.

Figure 3-1

Name _Megan_   Date _1-24-97_

Learning from One Another's Strategies

READ EACH PERSON'S STRATEGY. WRITE A COMMENT TO AT LEAST 3 OF THE FIVE PEOPLE. COMMENT ON:
- WHAT YOU NOTICE ABOUT THE STRATEGY;
- HOW THE STRATEGY IS HELPFUL; OR
- WHAT YOU APPRECIATE ABOUT THE STRATEGY.

Jessica: 12 R 1 / 6 ⟌73   I predict that each person will get 12 cents and you will have 1 cent left over. Each person gets one dime and two pennies with one penny left. (turning the problem into money in your head)

I think thats good saying money and not blockor units or longs.

Kimberly: 12 R 1 / 6 ⟌73   I predict that I am going to trade one long for 10 units because there are two reasons that I have to trade one long. One reason is that there aren't enough units to separate into 6 piles, and the second reason is that there are 7 longs and 6 people, so you have a long left.

I think thats a great mental dirsion problem.

Craig: 12 R 1 / 6 ⟌73   I predict that it will be 12 because 11 x 6 = 66, and I thought it would be 12, and there is one unit left.
My answer is 12 and 12 x 6 = 72 and you would have 1 left, but if you do it like this, then you would be 7 units over and 11 x 6 = 66. This is a little smaller than 12 x 6 = 72, and that is closer than 11 x 6 = 66, and 13 x 6 = 78 and the answer is 12 x 6 = 72 and 73 ÷ 6 = 12 R 1.

I like how you are multiplying to help you.

Megan: 12 R 1 / 6 ⟌73   I predict that you will have to trade one long in for 10 units because you don't have enough to go around twice. (6 longs and 13 units)

I like how I say that you can not go around twice.

Micah: 12 R 1 / 6 ⟌73   Each person gets one stick. Three of those people get the 3 units. Then split the stick into ten pieces that are left over and give them out and have a remainder of one unit.
I multiplied 6 x something that was in the tens. I knew 13 was too high, and 11 was too low. So I multiplied 12 x 6 and added 1 (12 x 6 =72, and 72 +1 = 73)

I like how you said nature for blocks.

We try to select entries that reflect a range of language and solution strategies. We also try to include samples from children who are either shy in class or who lack confidence in their mathematical ability. For this particular sheet, the children were expected to comment on any three of the five entries. They could base their comments on any of these ideas:

> What do you notice about this strategy?
> How is this strategy helpful?
> What do you appreciate about this strategy?

Afterwards we cut the responses from each sheet and gave them to each of the authors. We implemented this strategy because we wanted to make public more of the children's ideas, and we wanted everyone to take the time to look closely at the work of others. Obviously not everyone is as actively involved in class discussions, but the response sheets require everyone to take a stand.

Kimberly's solution that was printed on the sheet read:

$$\begin{array}{r} 12 \text{ R}1 \\ 6\overline{)73} \end{array}$$

> I predict that I am going to trade one long for 10 units because there are two reasons that I have to trade one long. One reason is that there aren't enough units to separate into six piles and the second reason is that there are 7 longs and six people, so you have a long left.

She received a variety of responses:

> I like how you told the two reasons. (Joshua)

> I appreciate how you said it so clearly and gave reasons why you have a long left. (Micah)

> I liked how you proved that you have to trade. (Lauren)

These are helpful appreciations to a mathematical writer: give reasons for your thinking and prove your point in a logical way.

Jessica used the context of money to solve the division problem:

> I predict that each person will get 12 cents and you will have 1 cent left over. Each person gets one dime and two pennies with one penny left.

She received numerous appreciations about that strategy:

> I like how you changed the problem into money because it's easier. (Lauren)

> I like how Jessica turned the problem into money in her head. I never thought of that before. I bet you could use this strategy for big numbers, too. (Joseph)

We discussed how sharing 7 dimes and 3 pennies among 6 people was a helpful way to think about this problem. Joseph wanted to extend the strategy by applying it to larger numbers. As we continued to work on long division problems, we took his advice and used the context of money to think about other problems, i.e. 734 divided by 5 could be interpreted as, "How would 5 people divide fairly 7 one hundred dollar bills, 3 ten dollar bills, and 4 one dollar bills?" Thus, responding to each other's strategies often highlighted useful ways of thinking that we all could consider.

Sometimes the use of response sheets prompted children to make comparisons with their own strategies. For instance, in another class William noted a similarity between the strategy that Rett used and the one that he employed (Figure 3-2).

Figure 3-2

Rett:
$$\overset{54\ r\ 0}{6\overline{)324}}$$

First I put 3 flats, 2 longs, and 4 ones and I had to divide them up into 6 people. Right when I looked at the problem I knew I would have to trade for longs and then I knew that I would have to trade 2 longs for twenty ones. After that I gave everybody an equal share. Everybody got five longs and 4 ones and there was no remainder.

Rett: I like how you did the problem and how did you know by looking at the problem that you needed to trade 2 longs for twenty units. I've done a problem like this when my mom gave me this problem— 5)475 I looked at it and I knew that I couldn't give 5 people 1 flat.

For the problem, 324 divided by 6, Rett wrote:

$$\overset{54\ R0}{6\overline{)324}}$$

First I put 3 flats, 2 longs, and 4 ones, and I had to divide them into 6 people. Right when I looked at the problem I knew I would have to trade for longs, and then I knew that I would have to trade 2 longs for twenty ones. After that I gave everybody an equal share. Everybody got five longs and 4 ones, and there was no remainder.

William commented:

I like how you did the problem, and how did you know by looking at the problem that you needed to trade 2 longs for twenty units. I've done a problem like this when my mom gave me this problem: 475 divided by 5 . I looked at it, and I knew that I couldn't give 5 people 1 flat.

William observed that both the division problems required trading the hundreds immediately: 324 divided by 6 and 475 divided by 5. It is interesting that he recalled this problem from a homework session that he had with his mother. Learning is making connections, and these response sheets enabled learners to make connections across problems and see new patterns and relationships.

In another example, Rett saw that he and Nikki used a similar strategy in multiplication, but they just described it in a different way. Nikki solved the problem of 24 x 5 = ? by drawing a diagram (Figure 3-3), demonstrating the area model of multiplication.

Figure 3-3

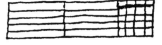

Writing about Multiplication

Nikki: How I got the answer was that I had on one side there is 5, then across there is two tens, so that equals 20. So I did 5x20 and it equaled 100. So then I went to the ones side and there was 5 on one side and 4 across so then I put 5x4= and it equaled 20. So I did 100+20 since those were the two answers.

24 x 5 = 120

5 x 20 = 100 +
5 x 4 = 20
120

She wrote:

> How I got the answer was that I had on one side there is 5, then across there is two tens [expanded notation 20 + 4], so that equals 20. So then I went to the ones side and there was 5 on one side and 4 across, so then I put 5 x 4 = and it equaled 20. So I did 100 + 20 since those were the two answers.

$$24 \times 5 = 120$$

Rett had solved the problem, 34 x 3, by drawing a line to separate the tens and ones:

$$\begin{array}{r} 34 \\ \times\ 3 \\ \hline 102 \end{array}$$

He described his strategy in this way:

> I did the first problem by imagining that there is a line between the three in 34. Then the 3 under the 4 tells me how many thirties there will be [3 x 30 = 90]. Then I times 3 x 4. [90 + 12 = 102] Then I had my

answer, one hundred and two. . . .It is a lot easier doing these kind of problems with my strategy. I wonder if we had problems with higher numbers, would it be harder or easier?

When Rett read about Nikki's strategy, he saw a connection to his own strategy, and he wrote the following reply to Nikki:

I and Nikki have sort of the same kind of strategy except I imagine that there is a line to make it easier. I liked when Nikki said I did 5 x 20 to not make it so hard, and that is when I thought that I and Nikki had similar strategies.

Both children used the distributive property which we had discussed in class. They also computed the number of tens and hundreds first, and then added the ones. Although this procedure was not the traditional approach of moving from right to left, the students chose it because it was efficient and made good sense to them. Nikki drew a picture to show how 24 could be viewed as 20 + 4, while Rett used a vertical line through 34 to show that it was composed of 3 tens and 4 ones. In this way, Rett gained a new perspective on his own strategy. It is this public sharing of strategies, in both oral and written form, that provides a forum for validating diverse responses and inviting self reflection.

Valuing Nontraditional Solution Strategies

Part of developing a personal voice in mathematics is having the freedom to adapt as well as invent alternatives for solving problems. For instance, many of our children computed right to left, partly because that was the way the trading game worked and that was the way they had been taught in previous grades. However, we continued to emphasize predicting so that students would look at the problem in a more global way and decide for themselves what would make the most sense. For instance, in the problem: 345 – 116 many children subtracted the hundreds first, and then did the exchanging for the tens and ones. When we asked them why they started with the hundreds first, they said, "I could see there is no trading with the hundreds, so I did that first." Conversely, when confronted with the problem: 765 – 182 many children subtracted the ones first, and then did the exchanging for hundreds to tens. Here again their strategy was to begin the problem where they saw that exchanging was not necessary. It is this flexible use of the exchanging process that gives students ownership and responsibility for their own thinking.

Nikki demonstrated the procedure of moving from left to right when solving 67 + 58. She wrote:

I traded my 67 and my 58 into a hundred square and then I took the 7 and the 8 and traded them into a stick of ten. I put 6 and 5 sticks of ten, and that equaled 100 but I had 1 extra [ten]. . . . So that is 1 hundred and 1 [ten]. Then when I had those two numbers, 7 and 8, well, I put the 2 of the little cubes to the 8, and that equals 10, so I traded that 10 for a stick of 10, so that equals 1 hundred and 2 tens. I had 5 left, and that equals 125.

Here Nikki computed hundreds first, then added ones, and finally tens. She remembered that her two tens were the result of two different exchanges. Another student, Rett, sometimes used this left to right procedure and wrote that it required "a lot of switching around" (in this case, the number of tens changed from 1 to 2 after the ones were exchanged). Although this procedure may seem cumbersome to adults, it made good sense to the students. We shared Nikki's strategy with the class because we wanted to honor this alternative strategy and encourage other students to blaze mathematical trails that were nontraditional.

Ryan used a mental computation strategy to solve $213 - 147$ (Figure 3-4). As he described in his writing he "pretended" that 147 was really 113, and subtracted $213 - 113 = 100$. However, he knew that subtracting 113 was not enough, so he mentally subtracted $47 - 13$ and found "47 is 34 more than 13, $100 - 34 = 66$." When asked how he knew that $100 - 34 = 66$, he replied, "I subtracted $100 - 30$, and that's 70, and then take away 4 more, and that's 66." We asked Ryan what his strategy reminded him of, and he mentioned the connection to Humpty Dumpty. We urged him to draw a picture of this metaphor in his journal. He later described his illustration in this way: "He's just sitting on the wall with 213 - 147. Then he swerves and falls off, and then he turns into $213 - 113$. Then all the king's horsemen and all the king's men try to put his head back together again, and that's $213 - 147$. The king has 34 in his hand and he's putting it back in there (in the broken egg). There's 113, and he puts the 34 back in, and then it's 147."

This metaphor placed a personal signature on Ryan's math-ematical thinking but also provided a social invitation for others to use this strategy in new ways. In fact, later in the year Sara noticed that she could transform 66 X 2 into 33 X 4 and get the same answer. She remembered that Ryan split up numbers in different ways to find his answer in subtraction. She connected his strategy to her discovery in multiplication, and remarked, "It's sort of like Humpty Dumpty." It is this kind of exploration that teachers can foster by encouraging students to : (1) solve problems in different ways; (2) create metaphors that provide a rich pool of mathematical images; (3) and share their thinking with the class so that others can use and adapt these ideas in new ways.

Another example of a nontraditional strategy occurred when Scott solved 324 divided by 6 (Figure 3-5).

Figure 3-4

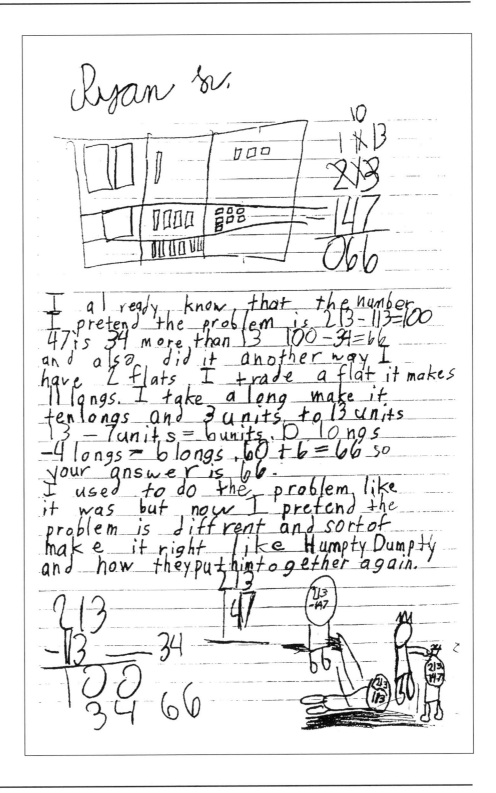

Ryan sr.

10
1 × 13
2 × 13
47
066

I already know that the number pretend the problem is 213 - 113 = 100
47 is 34 more than 13 100 - 34 = 66
and also did it another way I
have 2 flats I trade a flat it makes
11 longs. I take a long make it
ten longs and 3 units to 13 units
13 - 7 units = 6 units. 0 longs
- 4 longs = 6 longs. 60 + 6 = 66 so
your answer is 66.
I used to do the problem like
it was but now I pretend the
problem is diffrent and sort of
make it right like Humpty Dumpty
and how they put him together again.

213
-13
100

- 34
34

213
47

213
-147

66

Figure 3-5

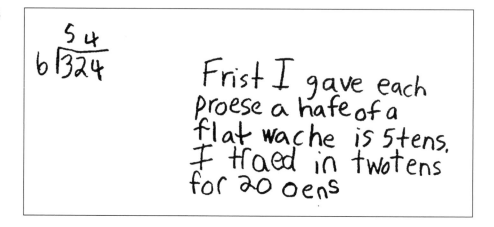

Scott wrote: "First I gave each person a half of a flat, which is 5 tens. I traded in two tens for 20 ones." When he tried to distribute 3 flats (hundreds) among 6 people, he realized he couldn't, but then re-marked, "I could give each person half of a flat." David said, "Good, Scott. And how much is half of a flat worth?" "Fifty," he replied, and wrote a 5 to placehold that part of his answer. He then exchanged tens for ones and divided 24 by 6 to complete the rest of the problem. The class tested out Scott's strategy on other problems where the first digit was half of the divisor, such as: 432 divided by 8 = 50 + 4 = 54 and 228 divided by 4 = 50 + 7 = 57. Although Scott was not a confident writer, we encouraged him to record his thinking by saying: "You've invented a strategy that no one in our class has ever thought of before." Valuing this kind of alternative thinking helps to honor the voices of all students.

Reflecting on Common Computational Miscues

The reader may be surprised to see the word "miscue" in a book about mathematics. We have borrowed "miscue," like "revision," from the field of language arts because it recognizes the thinking behind children's responses. Ken Goodman (1965) coined the term "miscue" to describe unexpected responses in reading. He wanted to look beyond what educators commonly called "errors" to better understand the sense-making efforts of learners.

One strategy that we use with children is to have them analyze common miscue patterns and examine the thinking behind them. For instance, a frequent miscue in long division is for children to omit a zero in the quotient (or answer) of certain problems. In the problem 515 divided by 5 it is common for some children to record an answer of 13, thinking 5 divided by 5 = 1 and 15 divided by 5 = 3. To analyze this miscue, we asked the class to write why it was necessary to record a zero in the quotient of 515 divided by 5. Their responses revealed some interesting descriptions and also served as a window into their own conceptual thinking about place value. Several children used a metaphor to describe the effect of not having a zero. Watkins wrote, "It makes sense to have a zero because if you did not have a zero the numbers would cave in. It is like a keystone on a bridge." Nick explained, "The zero holds that place like a bank that is bankrupt until you have enough to give to the bank to get it running again with money to give to everybody." As a keystone the zero needs to keep the other numbers of the quotient in their proper place value order, or they will cave in and become one new number. As a state of temporary bankruptcy the zero represents that there are simply no tens to distribute. Both images contribute new perspectives to the class' understanding of the division process.

Other children argued that number sense alone would dictate that there had to be a zero in the quotient: "It does make sense to have a zero because you have to have at least 100 [in your answer]" (Tiff); and "It makes sense to put a zero because if you did not you would get a totally different answer. Like if you were supposed to get 103 you would probably get 13, and that would mess up the whole problem" (Stephanie). These children emphasized in their own way that zero is a place holder that makes their answers more reasonable.

When Kimberly wrote, "I realized I would have to trade a long because there are 5 people and 1 long" she was helping us see that zero occurs in the quotient when the divisor (5) is greater than the number in the dividend (1). Lori explained this same idea in a different way: "We don't have enough longs to give to the people, so I put a zero on top of the 1 (in 515) because nothing happened." In this explanation, Lori used a zero to represent that no partitioning of whole tens was possible. Thus, all these explanations gave the class a rich pool of descriptions and logical reasons to overcome this common problem in long division. It is these kinds of conversations that demonstrate to children that the "warrant" for following certain mathematical procedures "comes from mathematical argument and not from a teacher or a book" (Lampert, 1990, p. 44).

A second strategy that we have used to address common computational miscues is more playful in nature. One example took place after the children had practiced problems in subtraction that have zeros and require exchanging. David purposefully wrote and solved the following problem on the board:

$$\begin{array}{r} 507 \\ -164 \\ \hline 403 \end{array}$$

He then asked, "What kind of advice, if any, would you give me after looking at what I have done?" The children enjoyed having an audience for their writing, and they also revealed their understanding of place value in their explanations. Some children knew right away the source of the difficulty. Jacqui advised, "The ones place is good because $7 - 4 = 3$, but the tens—that's a whole other story . . . . He put down a zero because he flipped out!" Nia offered another explanation for David's miscue: "The tens answer is wrong because you were thinking it was times, and that is how you got 0, and you forgot to regroup." Any number multiplied by zero is always zero, and children sometimes apply this understanding to subtraction problems. Nia's writing helped to show another common problem that we teachers might have overlooked, i.e. overgeneralizing the multiplication of zero. Other children wrote more direct instructions: "Keep practicing. And $0 - 6$ cannot go together, so you got to take away one of the hundreds" (Amber). Amanda embellished her response with a drawing of a disgruntled David standing next to the problem $1009 - 661 = ?$, which she humorously labeled "Dr. D's (David's) Worst Nightmare," since it is composed of even more zeros!

Another benefit of these written responses became apparent when several of the children either approved of his faulty solution ($507 - 164 = 403$), or made additional miscues themselves. These new miscues informed our teaching, and we later gave those children some additional assistance. Among these responses were ones such as: "I would say, yes, it's right, because if you have zero and you have to take 6 but you can't take 6, it would be zero because I don't think there is another answer" (Andrea). Adam suggested that David exchange one of the hundreds, but then told him to exchange one of the tens as well (although he did not actually use the ten). He showed his new solution this way:

$$\begin{array}{r} 9 \\ 4\cancel{10} \\ \cancel{507} \\ -164 \\ \hline 333 \end{array}$$

Thus, by having children respond to common computational miscues teachers can better understand the thinking of their students, and plan next steps to help them in their understanding of this place value concept.

Writing Our Own Story Problems

Although base ten blocks are a useful tool for demonstrating the process of exchanging and the concept of place value, it is equally important that children have regular opportunities to apply these insights to a variety of real-life contexts. One strategy is for students to write their own story problems for their classmates to solve. On this occasion, we asked the children to write about the strategy they used to solve each problem because we wanted them to be more reflective about their problem-solving efforts (Figure 3-6).

Figure 3-6

Name _____   Date_____

Student-Authored Problems

Solve each problem, and WRITE ABOUT WHAT STRATEGIES YOU USED TO SOLVE THE PROBLEM.

1. (Sharnise) Sally had 65 pieces of string. She had to share it with 5 people. How many strings will each person have?

My strategies to solve the problem:

2. (Nathan) A magical cat travels into 7 different centuries. He buys 180 things from each century. He puts them in groups of 9. How many groups are there?

My strategies to solve the problem:

3. (Jacqui) There are 62 kids in Dean's class. Five kids were absent. The   teacher divided the kids up into 8 groups. Will there be any left over? How many groups?

My strategies to solve the problem:

4. (Jake) There are 23 people in Wade's class. If he wants to get everybody 3 candy bars each, how many bars does he have to buy?

My strategies to solve the problem:

5. (Casey) There were 30 cookies in the cookie jar. There are 4 of us in the family. The dog, Ebony, gets the leftovers. How many cookies do we each get, and how many does Ebony get?   (Solve and write about your strategies on the back)

By asking them to analyze their solution strategies, we were placing an emphasis again on sense making. Regular opportunities to defend their thinking makes learners more critical problem-solvers. However, when we read their papers the next day, we found that even many of the children who got the problems correct, merely listed the steps they followed without any explanation of why those steps made sense. For example:

> *Problem:* A magical cat travels into 7 different centuries. He buys 180 things from each century. He puts them in groups of 9. How many groups are there? (written by Nathan)

> *Response*: Multiply 180 x 7, divide 1280 by 9, and get 140. (Ryan).

> *Problem:* Sally had 65 pieces of string. She had to share it with 5 people. How many strings will each person have? (written by Sharnise)

> *Response:* I divided because you can't do anything else. (Alan)

We did not want their answers to sound like "choose the right operation," but rather to reflect their thinking process. Frustrated, we placed the children with partners, gave them each a new sheet of the same problems, and asked them to help each other by explaining the reasons for their actions. Phyllis said to the class, "Sometimes talking helps writers make sense of what they are trying to say. That's why we hold author's conferences. When you read your stories aloud you can hear your own words, and then check if it sounds clear, makes sense, and has proper punctuation. Talking helps us in all the writing that we do."

The children's second try at explaining their strategies showed a marked improvement in most cases. For instance, Ryan's revised explanation read, "You times first because you have to see how many you have in all. Then you have to group them so you divide." He cited reasons for both his actions. Casey wrote clear justifications for her actions as well (same problem): "First you have to times 180 x 7 which tells how much he bought all together, which is 1260. You have to divide to show how many groups the magical cat can put them in." Sometimes this strategy of writing with a partner helps children add more details to their explanations.

After having the children work with partners to solve these problems, Phyllis asked them to write in their journals about their collaborative work. Jacqui wrote: "Nia and Chrystal helped me with #2 by showing me the three steps. They showed me how to figure out the problem and I solved it on my own. Now I can explain it much better with three steps." Nia and Chrystal acted as mentors for Jacqui, who then was able to solve that problem on her own. She was learning that with help from others she could accomplish tasks that were just beyond her reach when she worked independently (Vygotsky, 1978). Casey realized that even without her peers nearby, she could still use talking to help herself express her thoughts: "The hardest problem was Nathan's problem probably because it was two or three steps. I knew how to do his problem, but it was hard to put it into words. Now I talk in a light voice (i.e. quietly to herself) and write what I say." Talking was a useful tool for Casey to get her writing started. By writing about that strategy Casey validated for herself the importance of what she was doing.

More Story Writing: Exploring Personal Contexts for Ten

Another strategy for creating contexts for computation begins with brainstorming personal contexts for sets of ten. Children can often show insightful mathematical thinking about place value and exchanging when it is tied to a familiar context. "What comes in sets of ten?" we asked the children. They suggested such items as pencils, marbles, stickers, dimes, baseball cards, tangerine sections, and packs of candy (especially Kit Kat bars). We then asked the children to create stories using these items to solve the problem:

$$\begin{array}{r} 83 \\ -28 \\ \hline \end{array}$$

This invitation was slightly different from the previous story writing assignment in that the author had to describe both the problem and the solution in the story. Their writing revealed some interesting strategies.

Nikki used the popular context of candy to write her story.

> I had 3 Kit Kat bars, and I had to give some away, and I had to subtract from 8, and I couldn't, so I went over to the big stack of Kit Kats and got 10, so then I had 13. So then I subtracted 13 – 8, and that equaled 5. So then I went over to the tens place, and I saw an 8 and a 2, but since I had to take 10 away, and that made 7 packs of Kit Kat bars, so then I had to subtract 7 – 2 = 5. So that's how I ended up with 55.

She described the exchanging as the process of breaking open a pack of Kit Kat bars; she also explained why she subtracted 7 – 2 in the tens column rather than 8 – 2. We had highlighted this common miscue earlier in the year, and Nikki chose to include that detail in her writing. Group conversations influence the kind of writing that individuals do.

Brent solved the same problem using a mental computation strategy that involved the context of pencils. He wrote: "I had 83 pencils. I had to give Sam 28 but I did not have enough out of a pack. So I took three whole bags. I gave him [Sam] all of them and he gave me two [individual pencils] back." Brent started to subtract tens first by giving away more than was required (we related this strategy to paying for items in a store). Brent explained that 83 – 30 = 53, but the two he received back made his final answer 55. The familiar context of breaking apart a pack of pencils supported Brent to invent this alternative problem solution.

Rhiannon used bags of marbles to illustrate the problem, 83 – 28 (Figure 3-7).

Figure 3-7

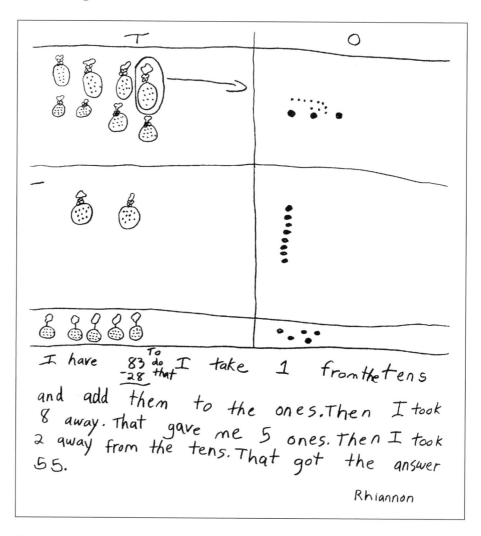

She used an arrow to designate the exchanging and different size dots to show the newly-distributed marbles. Rhiannon capitalized on her interest in drawing to represent this subtractive process. It is this variety of problem generation and solutions that values individual voices and continues to support personal inventiveness.

Conclusion   In this chapter, we have discussed the role of talking and writing in developing mathematical understanding about number operations. Despite the value that we place on these tools for expression, we face a challenge as teachers. We know that we have a limited amount of time, and we can't have children talking and writing about everything. So how do we choose what to pay attention to and what to ignore? There is no easy guideline to follow; teachers know their children best and must decide what to do based on numerous factors, such as the individual child involved, the nature of previous conversations about this same topic, the potential for generating further mathematical understandings, etc. However, some of the criteria that guide our decision making include these: Is this child taking a risk, sharing a surprise, describing a new strategy, building on the ideas of others, or suggesting an extension? If we can say yes to one or more of these questions, then it is likely we will extend this experience further. We look for opportunities that can uplift individual voices, advance the group's mathematical thinking, and build a safe and supportive mathematical community. Sometimes the experiences that we choose to discuss are planned by us in advance (why is it important to place a zero in the quotient?) while others arise unexpectedly (why was it important for Matt to write about his revision in thinking?). Living with this tension of the planned and the spontaneous is part of what it means to be a reflective teacher.

In this chapter we have tried to highlight the teacher's role in building a community of learners who value the process, honor surprise, benefit from reflection, and recognize the thinking of others. We have shared numerous strategies that have been helpful in promoting these norms: (1) sharing strategies together (such as addition strategies for playing the trading game); (2) discussing predictions and observations about computational problems; (3) analyzing common computational miscues; (4) drawing out children's language for describing mathematical ideas; (5) bestowing appreciations for each other's thinking; (6) highlighting a diversity of responses that includes not only different solution strategies but also different ways to represent those solutions; (7) valuing new directions (such as an interest in dividing odd numbers by even numbers); (8) inviting the creation of story problems with a familiar context; and (9) posing questions that value sense making and revision of thinking (Why does that answer make sense to you, and What helped you decide to revise your thinking?). In these ways we encourage children to think and reason for themselves, even in the area of computational algorithms.

4 Making Personal Connections to Geometric Ideas

Just as the teaching of algorithms is often simplified to a memorized list of procedural steps, so the teaching of geometry is often reduced to the transmission of terminology and definitions. We are certainly interested in having children learn to compute efficiently and accurately, and to learn important geometric vocabulary and concepts. However, we want to be sure that learners have the opportunity to make sense of these ideas in their own way. In this chapter, we describe several hands-on geometric activities. We want to stress that the value of these activities lies not in the manipulatives themselves, but in the thinking that the children demonstrate through their writing and talking. The role of the teacher is crucial in encouraging children to propose theories, build on the ideas of others, reflect on their own learning, and make detailed observations. When learners are given the opportunity to construct the understanding for themselves, they will raise intriguing questions, make unanticipated connections, and share their emerging theories. The interchange among students in this chapter emphasizes an important goal of "Mathematics as Communication" in the Standards: "Interacting with classmates helps children construct knowledge, learn other ways to think about ideas, and clarify their own thinking" (1989, p. 26).

In this chapter, we describe two geometric experiences. The first demonstrates the importance of trial and error in discovering important relationships among the sides of a triangle. It also highlights the value of children creating their own definitions for mathematical terms. The second experience shows the importance of comparing both geometric and numerical patterns. It also highlights the benefits of children explaining why some patterns do not emerge as they had expected.

What is a Triangle?

Textbooks often begin with definitions. Although definitions and technical vocabulary are important aspects of mathematical knowledge, we have found it more beneficial to begin with some engaging mathematical experiences. Later on, we invite the children to construct their own definitions by drawing upon insights gained from these initiating activities. One example of this strategy occurred when we challenged the children to investigate the properties of triangles in open-ended ways. For this first activity (Lindquist & Dana, 1980), we gave them a set of strips of paper that were 3–15 cm in length (Appendix 3). They cut out these lengths and then placed any three of them together to make a triangle. They kept records of what they discovered along the way. One of the purposes of this experience was for children to explore the relationship among the three sides of a triangle. This relationship, known as the inequality principle, states that the sum of the two shorter sides must be greater than the length of the third side (i.e. if the sum of those two shorter sides were equal to the length of the third side, the result would be two straight lines). Although we wanted the children to discover this unique relationship, we planned the investigation in a way that would encourage a lot of predicting, collaborating and revising of ideas.

Sharing Initial Hypotheses

Early in the investigation the children found that not all sets of these lengths created a triangle. For instance, the lengths of 3, 4, 8 and 3, 7, 10 do not make a triangle. Many of the children seemed surprised by this fact. We encouraged them to record those unexpected discoveries and continue to investigate why these results were occurring. One of the benefits of this activity is that it highlighted the value of answers that don't work out. By valuing their problem-solving efforts and recording these unanticipated results, we were demonstrating that all information was useful, especially in the early stages of an investigation, when no one was sure where the results were going to take them.

After the children had cut the strips and experimented for about forty minutes, we came together to share some of their initial theories:

Brent: All three have to be close together. So 14, 15 and 3 might not work.

Jenny: The small one always goes on the bottom.

Danielle: If you take two little ones and a big one it probably won't work. It needs to be closer.

Chris: All evens usually work; all odds usually work. Big numbers and little numbers [together] don't work.

William: If you put all big numbers together, or littles together, it will work.

Cortney: You can't put two littles with a big.

Jenny: We know at one point that one strip gets too long, or one gets too small, and we're trying to find that out.

One of the features of this conversation is that much of it is tentative. The children used words like *might, usually*, and *probably* to convey the precarious nature of their current theories. However, sharing these new hypotheses honored individual voices, raised new ideas for others to consider, and built a spirit of risk taking. Polya (1954, pp. 7–8) reminds us that a key attitude for problem-solvers is the ability to say "'maybe' and 'perhaps' in a thousand different shades." In this way children see that even their tentative thinking is valued. As teachers we have found it important to recognize this tentativeness in conversation by saying, "I feel like this was a useful conversation because we all get new ways to think about a problem when people are willing to share their not-so-sure ideas with the rest of us."

Using Children's Ideas to Extend the Experience

The conversation raised a lot of issues for others to explore. As teachers we invited the children to consider some of these other ideas by asking, "Do odd and even numbers play a role in determining what combinations are possible? What about the range of the three numbers? Is there a limit to this range? Does it matter how the lengths are placed together (Jenny suggested the smallest length went on the bottom)?" Posing these kinds of questions demonstrates to the class that theories and ideas are proposed by individuals but are owned by the group. It is everyone's business to gather more information to confirm, reject, or modify existing theories. If someone finds a solution that does not fit a current theory, we examine that discovery and ask, "How does this information change our theory?" We debate and challenge ideas but never attack individuals. Over time children begin to see these values played out in classroom conversations and are more willing to take risks to share their partially-formed ideas.

Conducting a conversation part way through this investigation had several benefits. It gave children time to share promising leads, foiled attempts and new surprises. It also helped to summarize the results of the entire class. When we continued the investigation the next day some children pursued their initial exploration while others decided to explore one of the ideas suggested by another student. For instance, Amanda tested out Cortney's idea when she wrote: "I notice that Cortney was right, you can't mix two little ones up with a big number because it won't match." She then drew a picture to prove her point by representing lengths 4, 5, and 9 (Figure 4-1).

Figure 4-1

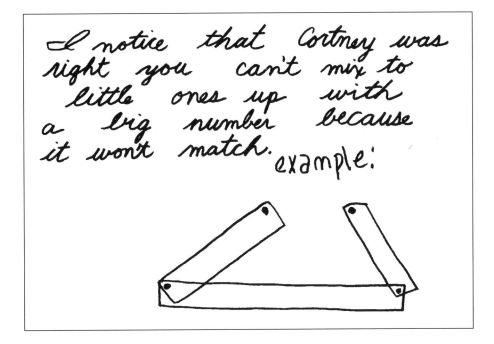

I notice that Cortney was right you can't mix to little ones up with a big number because it won't match. example:

Jonathan wrote about his first discovery: "I learned that if you pick three numbers that are three apart [he used 11, 8, 5] you could make a triangle." However, after the class-sharing session he decided to pursue a slightly different track: "I took most of my time working on Brent's theory [all three lengths need to be close together] and I might keep working on Brent's theory." He listed several sets of numbers that were close together and made triangles: 10, 11, 9; 11, 12, 13; 14, 15, 12. It is not surprising that he picked Brent's theory because that theory was related to his own. Like Amanda, he gave credit in his journal to another person's theory, reflecting the social norm of peer recognition.

Cortney tested out many of the theories that her classmates proposed. However, she still maintained her customary conversational style of writing as she did so (Figure 4-2). She began her journal by writing: "(1) What I tried is two little ones with one big one. The numbers I used were 4, 5, 12. Did they work out or not? They. . . do not. (2) Some people say that even numbers work on anything you do with numbers. You know, I'm going to try that. My numbers are 8, 10, 14. They. . . do! You know, maybe they're right. (3) I really don't like odd numbers so I'm going to try odd numbers. The odd numbers are 5, 7, 13. They. . . do not!" Since Cortney tested out only one example per problem, it was important for her to share her

Figure 4-2

1) What I tried is two little ones with one big one. The numbers I used were 4, 5, 12. Did they work or not? They ..... do not.

2) Some people say even numbers work on anything you do with numbers. you know I'm going to try that. My numbers are 8, 12, 14. They .... do! you know maybe there right.

3) I really don't like odd numbers so I'm going to try odd numbers. The odd numbers are 5, 7, 13. They ..... do not.

4) Now I'm going to try two odds one even. My numbers are 3, 9, 14. They ....

5) Now I'm going to try two evens one odd. My numbers are 4, 8, 15. They .....

Wonder ...	What if ...	Try out ...	Tried out ...
I wonder why evens worked with evens but not with odds.	What if we tried all the same odd numbers.		I tried all even all odd even and odd.

thinking with others (either in a small or large group) to see if they found similar results. In a mathematical community, there is this constant shuttling back and forth between individual and group discoveries as each shapes, and is shaped, by new thinking and emerging evidence. Cortney also developed a personal reflection chart at the bottom of her journal page that summarized what she had found out, what she was currently wondering, and what her next steps were going to be:

> Wonder . . . I wonder why evens worked with evens, but not with odds.
> What if . . . What if we tried all the same odd numbers.
> Tried out . . . I tried all even, all odd, [and] even and odd.

Cortney used our familiar classroom terms of *wonder* and *what if* to frame her current thinking. Her example serves as another reminder of the power of the words we use to describe the activities of our mathematical community.

A Second Sharing Time: Discussing Generalizations

When the children shared their thinking with each other for the second time they added some additional generalizations. Brent highlighted the process of his thinking by showing a chart of number combinations and wrote: "I notice that [the] closer they are the better they work" (Figure 4-3).

Figure 4-3

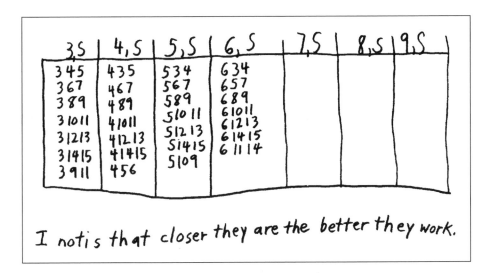

In his own succinct way he described the most obvious solutions for making a triangle. His chart (as well as Cortney's) helped show his peers another way to organize information. Here again, charts and drawings helped to highlight the process of their thinking just as much as their writing.

Several children offered generalizations to explain the overall findings. Chris wrote in his journal and then shared with the class this insight: "I think that if you get a big number and two small numbers that add up to the big number, it will not work. I think that if the two little numbers add up to only *one* number more than the big number then it will work." In his own way Chris was explaining the inequality principle of triangular lengths. His underlining of the word "one" showed that he knew the critical point at which triangles would, and would not, be formed. (For example, lengths 5, 8, and 13 would not work because 5 + 8 = 13, but lengths 5, 9, and 13 would work because 5 + 9 is greater than 13.)

Rett explained this same generalization, as well as some other observations, when he wrote (Figure 4-4): "I think that numbers in a row will work because they aren't that much bigger than each other. I also think that if you use numbers that equal each other you will have to stretch them out so far you won't have a triangle—you'll have a straight line. I learned that numbers in a row will work like 13, 14, 15. And two small numbers, like 3 and 7, that equals ten, and if you use 3, and 7, and 10 that won't work because 3 and 7 equal 10." In addition to his observations about consecutive numbers Rett elaborated on Chris's generalization. He gave a visual description of the stretching required to make a triangle work and then cited a specific example of 3, 7, 10 to prove his case. We then discussed with the children how the other observations that the class had made about consecutive numbers, odd and even numbers, etc. would fit under this broader generalization about lengths. In summarizing the findings, the children found that any set of three consecutive numbers would work, as well as any combination of odd and even numbers, as long as the sum of the two shorter sides was greater than the third side. By classifying their discoveries in this way we honored all the contributions that the children had made.

Providing this time for children to share their findings and current hypotheses is crucial. An important role for the teacher is to make sure that children present mathematical evidence to support their argument. In this way logic and reasoning, rather than personal preference, support the children's conclusions. The class conversation also highlighted the messiness of exploratory investigations. Since it was not clear from the beginning what were the most important attributes to consider, the children shared a variety of possibilities: odd and even numbers, consecutive numbers, single or double digit numbers, or a particular range of numbers. They pursued each possibility, shared their results collaboratively, and developed a broader generalization. It was this posing of initial hunches, sifting through specific examples and forming this broader mathematical principle, that captured the spirit of what it means to think mathematically.

Reflecting on the Importance of Risk Taking

This opening activity with triangles also helped to build important mathematical attitudes that contribute to a supportive, collaborative community: (1) It led children to use the strategy of trial and error. All of the children got started by picking a set of three numbers and

Figure 4-4

Comments

Work	I think that	Dosen't work
13,14,15	numbers in a row will	7,3,10
11,10,15	work because they	7,4,11
5,6,7	aren't that bigger	6,7,13
3,4,5	than each other. I also	
6,7,8	think that if you use num-	
9,10,11	bers that equel each	
13,11,14	other ~~===~~ you	
3,4,6	will have to stretch	
3,4,7	them out so far	
7,8,9	you won't have a	

triangle you'll have
a straight line. I learned
that numbers in a row will
work like 13, 14, 15
and two small numbers like
3 and 7 that equels ten
and if you use 3 and 7 and
ten that won't work because
3 and 7 equel ten.

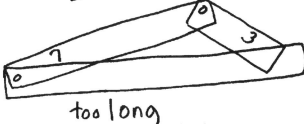

too long

seeing what happened. This strategy fosters a spirit of risk taking, i.e. I'm not sure if this is going to get me anywhere but I'll try it and find out. An important mathematical attitude is a willingness to persist in spite of these feelings of doubt. (2) It supported risk taking by highlighting the value of answers that did not work out. As teachers, we wrote on the board many of the combinations that did *not* make triangles. We asked the class to analyze all this information as they sought to discover a pattern or relationship. The availability of positive and negative examples gives learners more data to consider as they develop theories. Thomas Edison is reputed to have tried at least 1,000 different substances in his attempt to develop a filament for the first incandescent light bulb. An associate remarked that it was a pity that they had wasted so much time on materials that had failed, to which Edison replied, "Nonsense, we didn't fail — instead we now know one thousand substances that won't work" (McGavack & LaSalle, 1969, p. 24). It is this same view of knowledge that we want to cultivate in our classroom. Results that don't turn out as expected are also important data to consider. (3) The activity was open-ended enough to encourage a wide range of testing of ideas. Since there were so many possibilities to consider it was essential to collaborate and share our insights with each other.

Creating Their Own Definitions for Triangles

After this initial activity with lengths, we planned one other experience with triangles. We gave the children an assortment of plastic triangles and had them classify them in different ways. They also used these triangles to create a variety of patterns and designs. Following these experiences, we invited the children to write their own definitions of a triangle. They were encouraged to draw upon their insights from these beginning experiences to use in their definitions. Too often in mathematics children are handed the definitions of a textbook and never given the opportunity to create their own. Definitions are acts of classification. For instance, learners have to sort out significant attributes, such as having three sides, from irrelevant attributes, such as the size of the triangle or its orientation in space. By encouraging children to look closely and include important attributes in their own definitions, teachers can help their students make sense of these geometric ideas for themselves. By using their own language, students can place a unique personal signature on each of their definitions. We have also found that children record a variety of additional attributes that textbooks generally omit. For instance, children often emphasize that triangles can come in different shapes, and that any side can act as a base. A textbook definition of a triangle as a three-sided polygon does not include this information.

Sharing, Debating, and Personalizing the Definitions

After writing their definitions, we asked some of the children to share their ideas with the class. (Due to scheduling difficulties we conducted this activity when the girls were out of the room attending a health program.) Jonathan began: "What I put was, a triangle has three corners and three sides, and if you put a bottom line on a capital 'A' you would have a triangle."

As teachers we kept playing devil's advocate by raising other attributes not covered by the children's definitions. After Jonathan shared we gave appreciations for the attributes that he did include but then drew an open figure on the board (Figure 4-5a) and asked if that were still a triangle.

Figure 4-5a, b, c

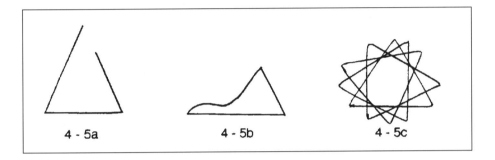

4 - 5a   4 - 5b   4 - 5c

Scott responded, "I wrote triangles had three sides, three corners, and it is not fully a triangle unless all sides are connected." Our counter-example had prompted him to add this last part to his definition. Although he had not yet written this additional information in his journal, we encouraged him to do so. In this way the conversation gave him the opportunity to extend his original definition and record further details in his writing. We then drew another shape (Figure 4-5b) on the board and asked if this were still a triangle. Eric responded, "A triangle has to have three straight lines. And I wrote that it's a three-sided shape; it has sharp edges and no curves. You cannot roll it, but you can make things with it, like a bunch of triangles can make a circle. And I drew it right here." He had spun a triangle around several times to show that it could spin into a circle, as in Figure 4-5c. We had engaged the students in an earlier experience in which they created a circle using a series of straight lines equidistant from a center point. It is likely that Eric drew upon this experience to show how a spinning equilateral triangle can create a circle.

William highlighted another aspect of triangles when he wrote, "Triangles come in all different sizes." When he shared this idea with the class, he added, "Also, don't worry, but if somebody doesn't know it's a real low, not a very big triangle, you could tell them that not all triangles come in the same size." He drew a stretched out isosceles triangle (with a long base and short height) to illustrate how different triangles can look. The diversity of shapes that are still considered triangles surprised William and many of the children, and he was able to validate that surprise by including it in his definition. Writing and talking about definitions after some initial experiences allows for personal reflection about what are the most noteworthy (and this often includes the most surprising) features of the shape.

Creating mathematical definitions also gives children the opportunity to connect personal interests to these terms. For instance, Kevin's interest in sharks led him to say, "If you drew a shark, you could see triangles on it . . . the teeth and the fin. The fin is bigger and the teeth are littler. And you could turn them and stuff. Like this one's up and this one is down (referring to the two rows of teeth). You can turn a triangle around." His personal example nicely connects to the previously-mentioned ideas about the rotation of triangles as well as their different sizes.

Both writing and talking help children explain their thinking. Chris wrote: "It has three sides and three corners. You can make it more than one way. It's two-dimensional. It is closed. It has angles. If you turn it, it will still be a triangle but it might not look the same. It has no curves." However, after reading this definition aloud to the class he thought that portions of his definition might not be clear. He therefore added this explanation: "And what I mean by, 'If you turn it, it might not look the same,' is if you have a triangle, like this (shows a picture he drew), and you turn it, it will look like this. But if you have a square, and turn it, it will still look like that. And a circle, if you turn it, it will keep looking like that. . . . And when I meant by 'you can make it more than one way'. . . you can make it like this, or like this (draws some triangles on the board) . . . really big, or long, or it could be like all even sides like this." Talking to an audience gave Chris the opportunity to expand his written definition by drawing examples on the board and contrasting triangles to squares and circles. Writers know more than they choose to record. By providing this sharing time teachers can give children the opportunity to revise their writing and explore their thinking further.

Sense making was at the heart of both of these mathematical experiences. Children used the strategy of trial and error to obtain some initial solutions. As they shared their results with peers, they were able to sift through positive and negative combinations to describe the broader generalization. They also used this experience to help them create personally meaningful definitions for a triangle.

Another way for children to make sense of mathematical ideas is to seek out patterns. Children must be encouraged to represent patterns in different ways, and analyze why those patterns are occurring. One interesting pattern that children can explore both numerically and geometrically involves square numbers.

Making Connections with Geometric and Numerical Patterns

We began our study of square numbers by reading *Sea Squares* (Hulme, 1991). This delightful book follows a predictable pattern told in verse. On each double-page spread, the number of creatures increases by one: one whale, two seagulls, three clown fish, and so on. Each of the creatures has a corresponding number of features, resulting in a total that is a square number: two seagulls with two eyes each make four eyes, and three clown fish with three stripes each make nine stripes. The pattern continues through $10 \times 10 = 100$. Talking informally after the story, the children noticed:

- Each successive page contained one more creature.

- The pattern involved multiplication ($7 \times 7 = 49$).

- Some numbers were odd and some were even (25 vs. 36).

- The book used rhyme, and some facts repeated sounds (five times five is twenty-five).

Defining a Square

Next, we asked the children, "Why do you think the author used the title, *Sea Squares?*" Their responses made it clear that they were not experienced with the term, square numbers. Their reasons for the title included such ideas as, "There is a square on the back of the book," or "There are squares in the borders on the pages." We also were not sure that the children really understood the properties of a square, since some had pointed to more rectangular shapes during the discussion. We therefore began our exploration by asking the children to define a square in their journals. As in the experience with triangles, we wanted to highlight what the children knew and to draw out their own descriptive language. However, in this case, we began with definitions because the children needed to understand the key attributes of a square in order to carry out the next investigation.

Some responses included:

A square is a shape that has four sides. You can turn it to a diamond shape and it's flat. (Ryan)

A square is a shape with 4 sides. It is a shape that will just stand still. It will not roll around. Sometimes squares have a hole in the middle, so you can put stuff in it like a box. A square also looks like an ice cube. (Whitney)

A square is an object that has 4 sides, 4 points, and one flat part. Like each side is one inch. The square has all equal sides like anyway you look at it, it has the same amount of room. (Maggie)

It was important to make the children's ideas public so that all of the class could benefit from the diversity of responses. Ryan's response alluded to the geometric concept of congruence; even if turned, squares are still squares. Whitney's description of "not rolling around" gave us teachers an opportunity to demonstrate how two squares can also stand next to each other, forming a straight line (90° + 90° = 180°). This demonstration emphasized the difference between right angles and acute or obtuse angles. Finally, we invited Maggie to discuss the property of equal sides for squares. Her definition was particularly important for the next activity that we teachers had planned. We intended to have the children construct squares of different sizes using one-inch squares from a standard pattern block set.

Beginning to Look for Patterns

Next, we returned to the story. "Let's look at the pattern of the numbers in the book another way," we suggested. We put one orange square on the overhead. "On the first page one whale had one waterspout." We then retold the next part of the story: "If two seagulls each had two eyes, all together there were. . . . " "Four eyes," responded the children. Next we invited a child to the overhead to create a larger square using four of the smaller squares. We talked briefly about how we knew it was a square (the same number of pattern blocks on each side). "How many of these square blocks would we need on each side to make the next biggest square?" we continued. The children suggested 3 x 3, and we built that square as well. When they counted the total in this larger square, they found that it corresponded with the page of three clown fish with three stripes each (3 x 3 = 9). The children were then ready for the challenge: "Build larger and larger squares, and record the total number of square pieces for each square in your journal. Write about what you notice or find interesting."

The children's journals showed how the visual experience of building larger and larger squares revealed numerical relationships as well. Many of the children noticed that it was easy to build the next bigger square by lining up tiles along two adjacent sides. Jennifer drew her diagrams of this pattern particularly well (Figure 4-6).

At first she noticed that the 2 x 2 square looked like a window. To make the next larger square, a 3 x 3, she added five more blocks. She said the arrangement of five more blocks looked like an "opposite L" (see Jennifer's arrangement of dots for her 5 x 5 square). The pattern of adding an "opposite L" of tiles made it easier to create larger squares. Inventing her own term, "opposite L," gave Jennifer a sense of ownership. Later, Jennifer shared her journal with the class, and both teachers and students adopted her term. During the activity, we asked Jennifer how she might highlight which blocks made

Figure 4-6

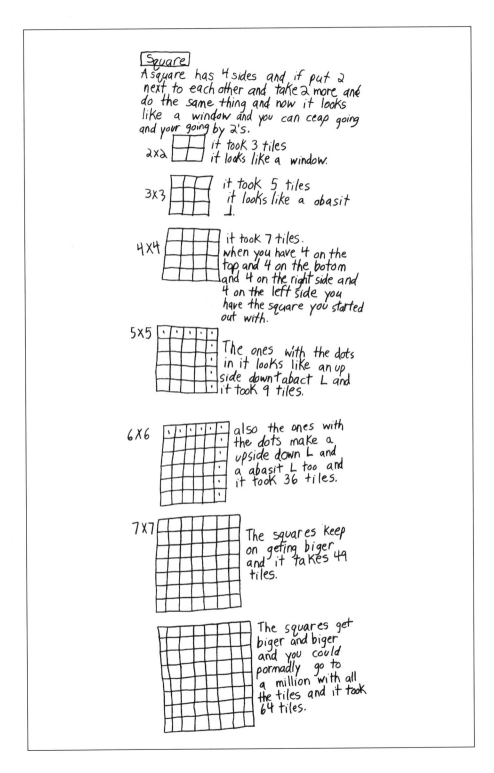

Square

A square has 4 sides and if put 2 next to each other and take 2 more and do the same thing and now it looks like a window and you can ceap going and your going by 2's.

2x2   it took 3 tiles
       it looks like a window.

3x3   it took 5 tiles
       it looks like a obasit
       L.

4x4   it took 7 tiles.
       when you have 4 on the
       top and 4 on the botom
       and 4 on the right side and
       4 on the left side you
       have the square you started
       out with.

5x5   The ones with the dots
       in it looks like an up
       side down abact L and
       it took 9 tiles.

6x6   also the ones with
       the dots make a
       upside down L and
       a abasit L too and
       it took 36 tiles.

7x7   The squares keep
       on geting biger
       and it takes 49
       tiles.

       The squares get
       biger and biger
       and you could
       pormadly go to
       a million with all
       the tiles and it took
       64 tiles.

an opposite L. Part of our role as teachers was to challenge students to find ways to represent their discoveries more clearly. Starting with 5 x 5, she highlighted this pattern by placing a dot on the diagram of each of the new blocks. We also noticed that Jennifer was able to develop her understanding of the properties of a square by creating, drawing, and writing about her discoveries ("4 on the bottom and 4 on the right and 4 on the left"). By the time she built an 8 x 8, she drew the conclusion that you "could probably go to a million." Jennifer saw that predictability was one of the benefits of finding a pattern.

AJ was another student who discovered this layering pattern (Figure 4-7):

Figure 4-7

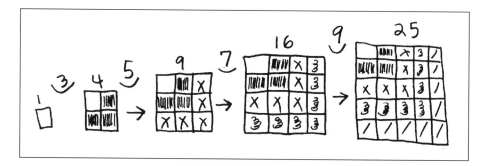

He invented a series of symbols to highlight the increasing pattern of squares. The work by AJ and Jennifer shows the value in encouraging a diversity of response. Jennifer's contribution to this investigation was her terminology, "opposite L." AJ's symbols preserved how each larger square was embedded in the previous squares. Both added to the class' collective understanding.

Summarizing Their Initial Findings

After some work time, we asked the children to stop and discuss their initial findings. We recorded the number of squares in chart form on the board:

Sides of square	Total number of tiles
1 x 1	1
2 x 2	4
3 x 3	9
4 x 4	16
5 x 5	25
6 x 6	36

"What patterns have you noticed?" we asked. Working together, most of the children had noticed the "opposite L." Studying the numbers on the board, several students commented that the total number of squares alternated between even and odd numbers. David then asked if anyone saw any pattern between the numbers 4 and 9, 9 and 16, 16 and 25, and so forth. After a few minutes of discussion, several children began to exclaim, "It's getting bigger by odd numbers!" They had discovered this important numerical pattern for square numbers:

$1 + \underline{3} = 4$ (square); $4 + \underline{5} = 9$ (square); $9 + \underline{7} = 16$ (square), $16 + \underline{9} = 25$ (square)

We added to the chart:

1 x 1	1	
		> + 3
2 x 2	4	
		> + 5
3 x 3	9	
		> + 7
4 x 4	16	

Children might use calculators to extend this pattern even further. The discussion highlighted the need for children to see patterns represented in different ways. Their drawings of the opposite L pattern helped them explain this numerical relationship that they found on the chart.

A Second Experience: A New Perspective on Square Number Patterns

For the next few weeks the children worked on multiplication in various ways. We then returned to the pattern blocks to revisit square numbers from a new perspective. Over a period of days we asked the children to try building larger, similar versions of each of the other shapes: green triangles, blue and tan parallelograms, red trapezoids, and yellow hexagons. It is possible to build successively larger triangles with triangles, parallelograms with parallelograms, and trapezoids with trapezoids. The numerical pattern of 1, 4, 9, 16 . . . also keeps appearing for these three shapes. However, it is *not* possible to build larger versions of the hexagon using only hexagons.

One of the purposes of this experience was for children to see that the same numerical pattern remained constant even though the shape of the figure changed. We also wanted them to confront the non-example (hexagon) and investigate why the pattern did not work with this shape. Mathematics has been defined as the study of patterns. Robert Davis says children must poke and pry into number patterns that lurk beneath the surface (Davis, 1964). We wanted children to not merely follow a pattern, but to delve beneath the surface and explain why that pattern was occurring. Although we teachers knew about many of the patterns that the children would discover, we did not know how the children would describe, represent, and personalize them. Therefore, we could not anticipate how their descriptions would lead the class in new directions.

Investigating the Pattern with Triangles

When the children built successively larger triangles, they were delighted to find that the numerical pattern remained the same (1, 4, 9, 16, 25, and so on). However, this time they were surprised to find that the new "layer" appeared horizontally across the base of each previous triangle. Emmanuel drew the pattern two ways (Figure 4-8).

Figure 4-8

I wonder why it is still shaped like a triangle.

His top sketch shows how the shape increased by horizontal layers of triangles. His larger figure shows how he would anticipate both the numerical and the geometric pattern to continue. Even though he saw the familiar 1, 4, 9, 16 pattern emerging, he was surprised by the new shape, and wrote, "I wonder why it is still shaped like a triangle."

Catherine described this same layering of triangles in another way. She compared the layers in the triangles to the pattern of horizontal lines in sedimentary rocks. When we read her journal, we were surprised and delighted by her comment. Catherine connected this geometric experience to an interest in rocks and minerals that the class had shown since the beginning of the year. Children continually brought rocks to school for observation and discussion. We had also conducted several experiments with rocks, including breaking sedimentary rocks into layers. Part of honoring mathematical voices is to listen to the personal connections that children make.

Continuing the Pattern with Parallelograms

The children's next challenge was to make larger versions of parallelograms. Again they found the same numerical pattern of square numbers. Jesse summarized all of these findings in his journal (Figure 4-9).

Figure 4-9

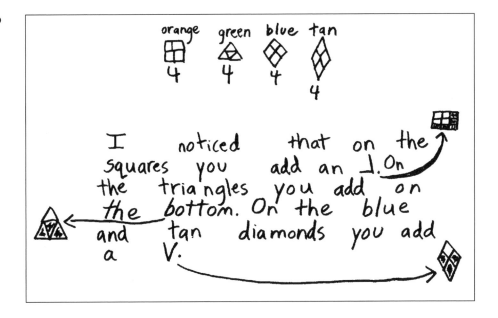

He was especially intrigued with the way each shape increased. He wrote, "I noticed that on the squares you add an L. On the triangles you add [layers] on the bottom. On the blue and tan diamonds you add a V."

Sara showed a different relationship among the shapes (Figure 4-10):

Figure 4-10

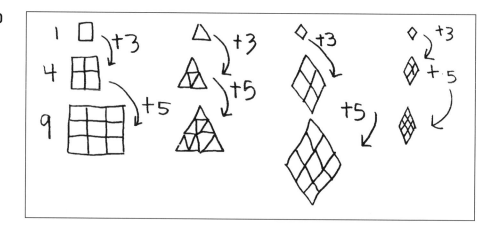

She highlighted the numerical growth of odd numbers across all shapes (1 + <u>3</u> = 4, 4 + <u>5</u> + 9, etc.). Her use of diagrams, numbers, and arrows succinctly conveys many of the main ideas of the investigation.

Gavin was fascinated with constructing larger and larger parallelograms. In fact, he gathered together some friends and made a large parallelogram of 100 pieces. Gavin had a chance to share this parallelogram when we paused to discuss findings midway through the investigation. Later, Cruz commented about Gavin's work in his own journal: "Gavin's pattern that I saw was a 10 x 10. They used 100 blocks to make it. There were 4 tens on the outside and it was 10 inches on each side. I found it interesting that they used 100 blocks." Cruz knew that writing about someone else's discovery was a legitimate response in his journal. The invitation, "What did you find interesting?" was not limited to just individual discoveries. Cruz personalized Gavin's findings by explaining the shape in his own way.

Testing the Pattern with Trapezoids

Finally, the children explored this same pattern with trapezoids. Although there were two solutions to this problem, (Figure 4-11a, b), the children were most interested in the solution shown in Figure 4-11a because it increased by successively larger "bridges." Gavin showed this solution in his journal (Figure 4-12). He wrote that "the trapezoids kept on having layers added to them." The children liked Gavin's arrangement because the layering followed a predictable pattern that was reminiscent of the L, horizontal, and V patterns of the other shapes. They described this layering as a "bridge pattern" because it reminded them of a bridge with supports. We also were intrigued with Gavin's closing comment that the problem was a difficult but rewarding task. For Gavin, writing was a way to record not only his findings, but his feelings.

Figure 4-11a, b

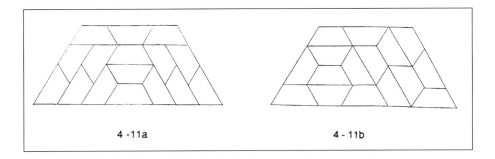

4 -11a   4 - 11b

Figure 4-12

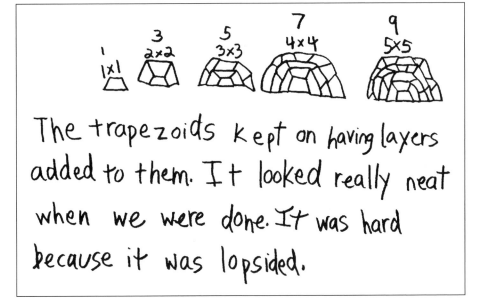

The trapezoids kept on having layers added to them. It looked really neat when we were done. It was hard because it was lopsided.

A Third Experience: Making Sense of a Surprise

In all of these experiences the children had found that they could enlarge each shape, and that each followed the same numerical pattern of 1, 4, 9, 16. . . However, when they tried to build larger hexagons with only hexagons, they found the task to be impossible. We felt it was important for the children to face this surprise for two reasons: (1) to see that some patterns do not always continue in a new context; and (2) to explain the unexpected in their own way. We asked the children to record their thinking about this hexagon puzzle in their journals.

Some of the children's entries included:

Hexagon[s] will never work because it has too many pointy edges. The yellow hexagon won't make its shape. If you add some it will just end up like a bathroom floor. If you keep adding it will never stop. (Sara) (Figure 4 - 13)

Figure 4-13

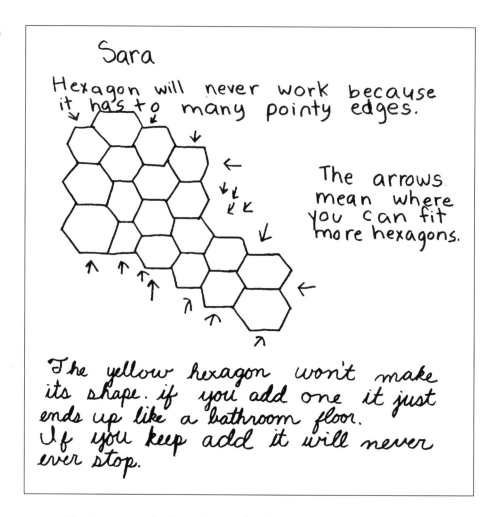

Sara

Hexagon will never work because it has to many pointy edges.

The arrows mean where you can fit more hexagons.

The yellow hexagon won't make its shape. if you add one it just ends up like a bathroom floor. If you keep add it will never ever stop.

The hexagons don't make another hexagon because it has lots of edges and you always have to keep going, and you'll never make a new one. The hexagons have lots of rough edges. .. You can always keep going. It is like the energizer bunny. (Whitney)

The hexagons do not work because every time you connect some of them it will have lots of room on the edges. (Selita)

A hexagon has so many sides you don't know what side to put the next hexagon in. (AJ)

The children wrote about their thinking in different ways. Sara related her experience of looking at tiled floors to explain that hexagons will "keep adding" and "never stop." Whitney used a metaphor (an energizer bunny) that was popular in the class to explain this same idea. She also wrote that the hexagons leave "rough edges," while Selita commented that hexagons leave "lots of room on the edges." AJ's comment that "you don't know where to put the next hexagon" highlighted that there is no L, V, or layering pattern to follow. Each student described this problem of edges in his or her own way.

Another Connection to Geology

Lastly, it was an additional journal entry by Sara that demonstrated to us the importance of leaving writing prompts open-ended. Like Catherine, who compared the layers of green triangles to sedimentary rocks, Sara connected her mathematical understanding to the class's ongoing study of rocks:

> I think it is neat that the blue diamonds can always make it [a diamond] bigger, bigger. But the hexagons don't make the same. It's kind of like breaking a rock because some rocks break into the same as the first one. And some don't.

Sara's comment amazed us. The children had seen a film about rocks where a geologist struck a large crystal, which broke into smaller pieces. Each piece was a miniature version of the original crystal shape. Sara knew that most rocks do not follow this predictable pattern of breaking apart. She used the concept of similarity to connect her geometric and geological experiences. Just as parallelograms can be enlarged to make larger parallelograms, so can some crystals be broken apart to make smaller crystal shapes.

As we thought back about Sara's analogy, we developed a new appreciation for the journal prompt, "What does this remind you of?" We had previously valued the prompt for the opportunity it gave children to express their thinking through their own language and connections. Now we saw new benefits of this prompt; it enabled children to make sense of a surprise, and to make new connections between mathematical and scientific ideas.

Conclusion

Children need regular opportunities to construct and explore geometric ideas. Writing, drawing, and talking in a collaborative community are important ways to go about this exploring. As children investigated the sides of a triangle, they shared discoveries, surprises, and current predictions. This interchange of ideas also gave children additional theories to test out. They took risks to share hunches and tentative conclusions. We recognized that this risk-taking attitude was an essential part of our classroom culture. In their writing they kept track of their findings, recognized the usefulness of others' ideas, and created their own mathematical definitions.

As the children explored square numbers, they found interesting patterns to describe. Their descriptions showed that how they represented patterns influenced what they could say about them. For instance, the numerical chart revealed the increasing pattern of odd numbers, while the geometric drawings prompted the descriptions of *opposite* Ls, *layers*, *V*s, and *bridges*. The writing prompt, "What does this remind you of?" inspired Catherine and Sara to make connections to sedimentary rocks and crystals. Their comparisons helped us teachers see more clearly the potential of this open-ended invitation. Other children used writing to explain the patterns and designs of other classmates. Lastly, we saw the importance of having all children write to explain an unexpected event (the hexagon puzzle). Multiple explanations enriched the class's collaborative understanding.

All of the experiences described in this chapter portrayed children as sense-makers. For children to own and apply mathematical ideas, they must first make sense of them—both individually and as a classroom community. In this chapter they made sense of mathematics by sorting examples from non-examples, sharing ideas collaboratively, uncovering patterns, connecting ideas through analogies, and explaining the unexpected. Writing, drawing, and talking became effective tools for the children to frame their current understandings and to make their thinking visible to others.

Conclusion

Some Final Thoughts on Talking, Writing, and Mathematics

The focus of this book has been respecting children as sense-makers. If sense making is at the heart of what we believe as educators, then reading, writing, talking, drawing, and doing mathematics become tools for expressing those sense-making efforts. We also know that teachers play a key role in fostering a classroom culture that values children's understanding and ways of thinking. To highlight this critical role we conclude this book by summarizing some of these important strategies.

Strategies for Supporting Talking and Writing about Mathematics

(1) Talk together about what you have discovered as a class. You might talk midway through an investigation as well as at the end. Record these observations on the board and encourage children to use them as beginning points for their own writing. Emphasize that writing is like talking on paper. Demonstrate that borrowing the ideas of others is not "cheating" but a legitimate way for writers to reflect about their own thinking as well as extend the ideas of others.

(2) Encourage drawings, sketches, and diagrams as worthy and informative journal entries. It is important for children to express what they know in many different ways.

(3) Ask open-ended questions to invite a range of responses. Good questions to start with include:

> What did you notice?
> What did you find interesting?
> What patterns do you see?
> What surprised you?
> What strategy did you invent that helped you with your investigation?
> What do your findings make you wonder about?

Glue these questions on the inside front cover of the children's math journals so that they can refer to them throughout the year. Invite children to add other questions to the list.

(4) Encourage metaphorical thinking by asking such questions as, "What does this remind you of? What does this look like? What picture does this make in your mind?" Metaphors invite personal connections as well as interdisciplinary ties, i.e. the layering of pattern blocks looks like sedimentary rocks.

(5) Use concrete materials regularly so that children have the opportunity to manipulate, visualize, and describe mathematical ideas.

(6) Support a wide variety of written responses. Some children develop a conversational style, while others write in a more analytical way. Some use drawings to explain their thinking while others prefer a more numerical approach.

(7) Provide time for sharing journals aloud. Invite children to offer *appreciations* for each other's strategies and insights. At other times, reproduce some journal entries, distribute the copies to each member of the class, and ask children to express their *appreciations* in writing.

(8) Give children the opportunity to publish their writing for different audiences. They might write directions for a math game that they invented, a summary of an interesting pattern for a hallway display, or a script for presenting a mathematical demonstration to some younger children.

(9) Use writer's workshop time as another opportunity for children to continue their mathematical writing.

(10) Reflect upon the benefits of a particular conversation by asking, "What did you find helpful about this conversation?" In addition, encourage children to share how the thinking of others gave them new insights and ideas: "Sara, it sounds like you're building off of Maggie's idea. Can you say something about that?" or "Who would like to explain how someone's idea helped them with their own thinking?"

(11) Emphasize sense making by asking, "How did you figure that out?" or "Why does that make sense to you?"

(12) Encourage children to elaborate on their thinking by responding, "Say some more about that idea," or "Tell us more about your thinking."

(13) Challenge children to cite mathematical evidence to support their reasoning: "How did you come to think this?" or "What other examples have you tested out?" Make public additional evidence by asking, "What information do other people have about this idea?"

(14) Support children not only to hunt for patterns but also to explain why those patterns are occurring.

(15) Solicit multiple solutions and strategies, as well as multiple explanations for the same idea: "Who solved the problem in another way?" and "Who else would like to explain this idea?"

Building a Supportive Classroom Culture

Another thrust of this book has been to emphasize the important classroom conditions that honor the mathematical voices of all learners. Some of these conditions, which have been reflected in the experiences described in this book, hinge on the decisions that a teacher chooses to make. Some of these key decisions include the following:

(1) Build in time to reflect on the experiences that make us a community. As teachers we need to take the time for the class to reflect on the little moments that make us a community: when one child credits another child for an idea; when children revise their thinking; when a shy child takes a risk and shares a current theory; when we help each other discover a pattern; when a child admits that she is confused and we help each other explain that confusion; when some of the class shows disrespect toward another member and we reflect about what that does to our community; or when a child borrows an idea of another student and extends it in a new way. It is often in these fleeting interchanges that the bonds of our classroom community are strengthened. If we are to grow as a community we must reflect on what makes us strong.

(2) Value mistakes as sites for learning (Hiebert, 1997). One way to establish this value is to ask questions about the process (whether the answer happens to be right or wrong). When teachers do this, they send the implicit message to children: I value your thinking and I respect you as a sense-maker. Often times children will revise their thinking when they have the opportunity to revisit what they have done. Teachers can also demonstrate the value of mistakes by encouraging children to share what they find surprising or confusing. In this way the unexpected becomes a site for analysis and exploration. Teachers also can view common computational miscues as opportunities to inquire. By doing so, the focus of attention is on explaining and understanding.

(3) Treat children differently (Ayers, 1993). This piece of advice for building a classroom community seems like a contradiction in terms. However, to establish an equitable classroom learners need to be treated differently in some regards. For instance, a teacher may want to encourage shy Sara to share her solution with the class. A teacher may want to push Ryan, who is quite proficient in math, to go beyond the data and extend the problem in a new way. A teacher may want to capitalize on Rhiannon's artistic ability by encouraging her to draw pictures of the exchanging process. It is through these individual responses of support that we build a community that has a richness of voices.

(4) Develop a language together that portrays children as constructors of their own mathematical knowledge. If we want to empower children to think for themselves, we call them "inventors," and ask, "Who can invent another way to solve this problem?" If we want to encourage children to search for patterns, we call them "detectives," and ask, "Is there a mystery, or puzzle, behind these numbers?" If we want to encourage children to reflect on their own thinking, we call them "authors," and ask, "Has anyone revised their thinking about this problem?" The language we use to describe the intentions of our classroom community define who we are as learners. How we describe ourselves sets the parameters for the risks we are ready to run, the questions we dare to ask, and the thinking we are willing to reveal.

Works Cited

Ayers, W. (1993). *To teach: The journey of a teacher.* New York: Teachers College Press.

Barnes, D. (1976/1992). *From communication to curriculum.* Portsmouth, NH: Boynton/Cook Publishers.

Borasi, R. (1991). *Learning mathematics through inquiry.* Portsmouth, NH: Heinemann.

Borasi, R., Siegel, M., Fonzi, J., & Smith, C. (1998). Using transactional reading strategies to support sense-making discussion in mathematics classrooms: An exploratory study. *Journal of Research of Mathematics Education,* 29 (3), 275–305.

Brown, S., & Walter, M. (1990). *The art of problem posing.* Hillsdale, NJ: Lawrence Earlbaum.

Cochran, B., Barson, A., & Davis, R. (1970, March). Child-created mathematics. *Arithmetic Teacher,* 17, 211–215.

Countryman, J. (1992). *Writing to learn mathematics: Strategies that work.* Portsmouth, NH: Heinemann.

Davis, R. (1964). *Discovery in mathematics: A text for teachers.* Reading, MA: Addison-Wesley Publishers.

Dee, R. (1988). *Two ways to count to ten: A Liberian folktale.* New York: Holt.

Eisner, E. (1991, February). What really counts in schools. *Educational Leadership,* 48, 10–17.

Goodman, K. (1965). A linguistic study of cues and miscues in reading. *Elementary English,* 42, 639–643.

Graves, D. (1983). *Writing: Teachers and writers at work.* Portsmouth, NH: Heinemann.

Hiebert, J. (1997). *Making sense: Teaching and learning mathematics with understanding.* Portsmouth, NH: Heinemann.

Hulme, J. (1991). *Sea squares.* New York: Hyperion.

Kamii, C., Lewis, B., & Livingston, S. (1993, December). Primary arithmetic: Children inventing their own procedures. *Arithmetic Teacher,* 41, 200–203.

Lakatos, I. (1976). *Proofs and refutations: The logic of mathematical discovery.* New York: Cambridge University Press.

Lampert, M. (1990, Spring). When the problem is not the question and the solution is not the answer: Mathematical knowing and teaching. *American Educational Research Journal,* 27, 29–63.

Lindquist, M. & Dana, M. (1980, March). Strip tease. *Arithmetic Teacher, 25,* 4–9.

Madell, R. (1985, March). Children's natural processes. *Arithmetic Teacher, 32,* 20–22.

McGavack, J., & LaSalle, D. (1969). *Guppies, bubbles and vibrating objects.* New York: John Day.

Mills, H., O'Keefe, T., & Whitin, D. (1996). *Mathematics in the making: Authoring ideas in the primary classroom.* Portsmouth, NH: Heinemann.

Murray, D. (1968). *A writer teaches writing: A practical method of teaching composition.* New York: Houghton Mifflin.

National Council of Teachers of Mathematics. (1989). *Curriculum and evaluation standards for school mathematics.* Reston, VA: National Council of Teachers of Mathematics.

Paulos, J. (1988). *Innumeracy: Mathematical illiteracy and its consequences.* New York: Hill and Wang.

Polya, G. (1954). *Induction and analogy in mathematics.* Princeton, NJ: Princeton University Press.

Pinczes, E. (1993). *One hundred hungry ants.* Boston: Houghton Mifflin.

Short, K., & Burke, C. (1991). *Creating curriculum: Teachers and students as a community of learners.* Portsmouth, NH: Heinemann.

Schwartz, D. (1985). *How much is a million?* NY: Lothrop, Lee, & Shepard.

Schwartz, D. (1989). *If you made a million.* NY: Lothrop, Lee & Shepard.

Schwartz, D., & Whitin, D. (1998). *The magic of a million.* New York: Scholastic.

Schwartz, S. (1996, March). Hidden messages in teacher talk: Praise and empowerment. *Teaching Children Mathematics, 44,* 396–401.

Steen, L.A. (Ed.) (1990). *On the shoulders of giants: New approaches to numeracy.* Washington, D.C: National Academy Press.

Vygotsky, L. (1978). *Mind in society.* Cambridge, MA: Harvard University Press.

Whitin, P., & Whitin, D. (in press). Exploring mathematics through talking and writing. In Burke, M. (Ed.), *Learning mathematics for a new century.* (2000 NCTM Yearbook). Reston, VA: National Council of Teachers of Mathematics.

Whitin, D., & Whitin, P. (1998). The 'write' way to mathematical understanding. In Morrow, Lorna (Ed.), *The teaching and learning of algorithms in school mathematics.* (1998 NCTM Yearbook) (pp. 161–69). Reston, VA: National Council of Teachers of Mathematics.

Whitin, P., & Whitin, D. (1997, February). Ice numbers and beyond: Language lessons for the mathematics classroom. *Language Arts, 74* (2), 108–115.

Whitin, D., & Wilde, S. (1992). *Read any good math lately? Children's books for mathematical learning, K–6.* Portsmouth, NH: Heinemann.

Whitin, D., & Wilde, S. (1995). *It's the story that counts: More children's books for mathematical learning, K–6.* Portsmouth, NH: Heinemann.

Wood, T. (1998). Alternative patterns of communication in mathematics classes: Funneling or focusing. In Steinbring, H. et al (Eds.), *Language and communication in the mathematics classroom.* (pp. 167–178). Reston, VA: National Council of Teachers of Mathematics.

Yashima, T. (1955/76) *Crow boy.* New York: Puffin.

Appendix 1

Introductory Activities with Base Ten Blocks

Free exploration
>Tell me about your design.
>What do you notice about the pieces?

Finding equivalences
>How many units make a long?
>How many longs make a flat?
>How many flats make a block?
>What do you notice about the answers to all these questions? How can you explain this?
>
>How many units make 4 longs?
>How many longs make 2 flats?
>How many units make 3 flats?
>How many flats make 2 blocks?

The trading game
>Make game boards divided into columns for units, longs, flats, and blocks. Take turns rolling a number cube and putting that number of units on your board. Players must always trade in ten of one kind of piece for the next largest piece whenever they can. When everyone makes a flat the game is over.
>One variation requires children to record their total on a long piece of adding tape. They continue to build the number on their board as well as write their new sum on the tape.

Show me
>Show me 12. What does the 1 stand for? What does the 2 stand for?
>Show me 204. What does the 2 stand for? the 0? the 4?
>Show me 666. What does each 6 stand for?

What's the difference?
>Build 54. Now build 45. They both have the same numbers. How are they different? Now try 32 and 23. How are they different? What other numbers could you try that look the same but are really different?
>Use the numerals 1, 4, 6 to build as many different numbers as you can. Build, sketch, and record all possibilities. How are these numbers different?

Change it
>Make 38. How can you change 38 to 48? Explain your thinking.
>Now let's try it.

Make 54. How can you change 54 to 60? Explain your thinking.
Now let's try it.
Make 62. How can you change 62 to 91? Explain your thinking.
Now let's try it.

Names for a number

How many different ways can you show 21 with your blocks? 53?
145? You might want to make a chart to show all possibilities.

Number riddles

I'm thinking of 6 pieces. Their value is less than 120.
I'm thinking of 4 pieces worth 31.
I'm thinking of 4 pieces worth 13.
I'm thinking of 7 pieces worth 142.
I'm thinking of 9 pieces. Their value is between 125 and 150.
I'm thinking of 8 pieces. There are twice as many units as flats.
I'm thinking of 5 pieces. Some are units, longs, and flats. Their value
is less than 300.
I'm thinking of 5 pieces that include 3 different size blocks. Their
value is greater than 30.
I'm thinking of 8 pieces. Some are longs, flats, and units. It is a
palindrome.
I'm thinking of 9 pieces. None are longs. Their value is greater than
400.

Appendix 2

Directions for Making Base Ten Materials

Teachers can make paper sets of base ten materials for their students. Copy the figures below using centimeter paper. Units can be made by cutting longs or flats. We enlisted the help of some parents who cut out and packaged sets of flats, longs, and units into zip-lock bags. The children used these paper sets to complete homework assignments. More durable sets can be made from card stock.

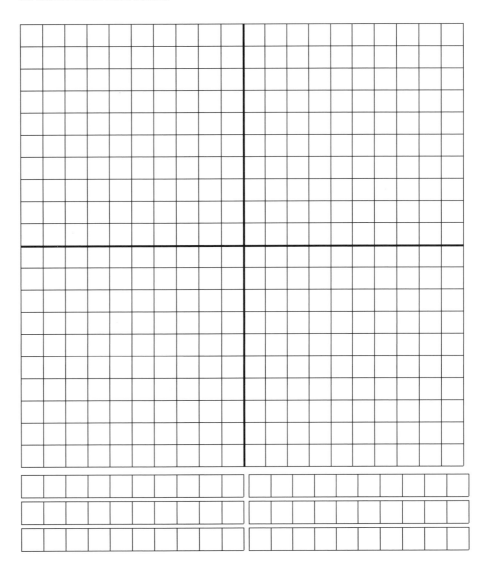

Appendix 3

Materials Needed for Constructing Triangles

Trace these strips on to card stock and cut them out. Try to construct triangles using any combination of three strips. Be sure that the dot on one strip overlaps the dot on a connecting strip (in this way the length of each strip is retained).

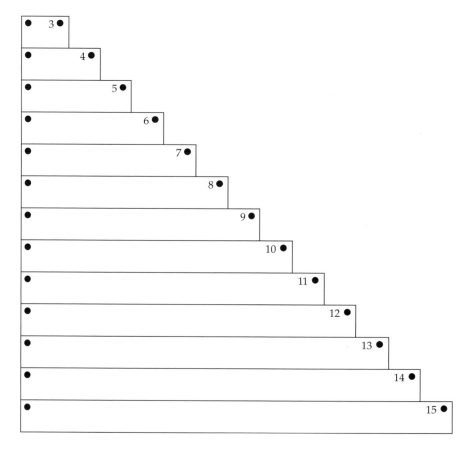

Authors

Phyllis Whitin teaches at Queens College of the City University of New York. Her wealth of teaching experience spans preschool through middle school and gives her a unique perspective on the issues of teacher research. She has had a long-standing interest in building a caring community of learners, developing an inquiry-based curriculum, and encouraging children to express their ideas in multiple ways. These interests are reflected in her books, *Sketching Stories, Stretching Minds* and *Inquiry at the Window*. She has also shared her fourth-grade classroom through the PBS Elementary Mathline Project. She is currently continuing her interest in classroom research by working with teachers in the New York City public school system.

David J. Whitin teaches at Queens College of the City University of New York. A former elementary school teacher and principal, he regularly collaborates with classroom teachers on ways to build children's mathematical understanding. He has always had a love for both language and mathematics. This dual interest is reflected in this book, as well as others that he has co-authored, including: *Mathematics in the Making, Read Any Good Math Lately?, It's the Story That Counts,* and *The Magic of a Million*. David and Phyllis did collaborative research in Phyllis's classroom for five years. Their first book, *Inquiry at the Window,* documents a yearlong, interdisciplinary study of birds. David is currently working with teachers in the New York City area to build responsive mathematical communities.

This book was typeset in Avant Garde and Palatino by Electronic Imaging.
Typefaces used on the cover and spine were Helvetica Narrow Bold, Officina Sans Bold, and Officina Serif.
This book was printed on 60-lb. opaque paper by Automated Graphic Systems, Inc.